The Nooch's Pooches Method
A Comprehensive Guide to Training and Living with Your Dog
Panos Anagnostou

Copyright © 2025 by Panos Anagnostou

The Nooch's Pooches Method: A Comprehensive Guide to Training and Living with Your Dog

All rights reserved. No part of this book may be reproduced.

This publication is designed to provide accurate and authoritative information in regard to the subject matter covered. While the publisher and author have used their best efforts in preparing this book, the advice and strategies contained herein may not be suitable for your situation.

You should consult with a professional when appropriate. Neither the publisher nor the author shall be liable for any loss of profit or any other commercial damages.

ISBN 978-1-7637780-0-9 (Paperback)

Edited by Shannon Clark

shannon@thementorscopywriter.com

Illustrated by Jane Stuart Art

jane@janestuart.art

Insta: @janestuarttatts

First edition 2025

Contents

Foreword	IV
Acknowledgements and Dedications	VIII
Introduction	IX
1. What it Means to Train Your Dog	1
2. Understanding the Theory of Dog Behaviour	5
3. The Fundamentals: Building the Foundations	31
4. Dog Training Definitions	63
5. Obedience Training	89
6. The Mindset of a Leader	179
7. The Structured Walk	189
8. House Manners: Master Your Castle	201
9. General Manners	241
10. Management is Key to Success	255
11. Socialisation	273
12. Behaviour Modification	285
Final Words	317

Foreword

It is with great pleasure and pride that I introduce this remarkable book by my dear friend, Panos Anagnostou. Over the past decade, I have had the privilege of witnessing Panos's evolution from a passionate newcomer in the field of dog training to a respected professional, devoted husband, and loving father. Our journey together began when he joined one of my dog training courses over ten years ago, eager to deepen his understanding and refine his skills. Little did I know that this initial encounter would blossom into a profound friendship built on mutual respect and shared values.

Panos is someone I can always rely on for his genuine honesty and unwavering integrity. His word is his bond, and his actions consistently reflect his deep commitment to ethical principles. In a world where sincerity can be hard to find, Panos stands out as a beacon of trustworthiness. He doesn't just talk about doing the right thing; he lives it every day, both personally and professionally. His roles as a wonderful husband and father only amplify his dedication to living a life of authenticity and compassion.

What truly sets Panos apart is his relentless dedication to personal growth. He constantly works on himself, striving not only to become a better trainer but also to enhance his own humanity. This commitment to self-improvement permeates every aspect of his life. Whether he's learning new training techniques, engaging in thoughtful conversations, or nurturing his family, Panos approaches everything with a mindset geared toward growth and understanding.

When Panos speaks, he speaks from the heart. He carefully considers his words, ensuring that his communication is both sincere and impactful. His ability to listen is equally profound. He engages with others with genuine interest, making those he interacts with feel heard and valued. This empathetic approach extends to his work with dogs, where understanding and patience are paramount. He doesn't impose his will but instead seeks to build relationships based on mutual respect and trust.

Panos' journey in dog training is nothing short of inspiring. Starting with his work with shelter dogs, he honed his skills in some of the most challenging environments. Working with animals that often had traumatic pasts, he learned the importance of compassion and resilience. This experience laid a strong foundation for his expertise and deepened his empathy for both dogs and their owners.

Building on this foundation, Panos took the bold step of creating his own business. He wanted to apply his unique philosophy and methods on a broader scale, helping more dogs and people build harmonious relationships. Not content to stop there, he also launched a successful podcast, sharing his insights and engaging with a global community. Through these endeavors, Panos has become a respected voice in the field, known for his thoughtful approach and willingness to tackle difficult topics.

Reading Panos' book has been a true delight. He writes with the same authenticity and conviction that he brings to his training and personal life. In this book, Panos addresses the real issues that dog owners face without shying away from the hard truths. He doesn't dance around topics that need to be addressed; instead, he confronts them head-on, providing practical advice and actionable strategies. His insights help dogs be at their best, and in turn, help owners understand their canine companions on a deeper level.

This book is more than just a guide to dog training; it's a reflection of Panos' philosophy and his commitment to fostering genuine connections between dogs and their owners. His holistic approach considers not just the behavior of the dog but also the mindset of the owner, emphasizing the importance of mutual respect and understanding. Readers will find that Panos' methods are both effective and compassionate, rooted in a profound respect for the bond between humans and animals.

In a field where trends come and go, Panos' work stands out for its depth, integrity, and heart. This book is a testament to his dedication as a trainer, a professional, and a family man. His experiences as a husband and father have only enriched his understanding of relationships, which he seamlessly translates into his work with dogs and their owners. I am confident that readers will find not only practical guidance but also inspiration in these pages.

It is an honor to call Panos a friend, and I am thrilled to share his wisdom with you. I trust that you will find his insights as enlightening and transformative as I have.

—Glenn Cooke

Acknowledgements and Dedications

Writing this book has been a journey of learning, reflection, and gratitude. There are many people who have played a part in shaping my understanding of dogs and their behaviour, and without them, this book would not exist.

To my family and friends, thank you for your unwavering support and encouragement throughout this process, your belief in me has been a guiding light. To the countless dogs and their humans I've worked with over the years, thank you for trusting me to help strengthen your bond. Each of you has taught me something valuable about the incredible relationship between dogs and their people.

To the mentors, colleagues, and trainers who have inspired me and shared their wisdom—your insights have been invaluable. Finally, to the readers of this book, thank you for taking this step to understand and connect with your dog on a deeper level. Your dedication to your dog's well-being is what drives this work.

This book is dedicated to the dogs who have been my greatest teachers and who continue to teach me the power of patience and love. And to all the dogs everywhere who continue to remind us every day of the beauty of trust, loyalty, and joy.

Introduction

My name is Panos Anagnostou, and I train dogs (and their owners) to live in harmony. My journey with dogs started over ten years ago when I volunteered at my local animal shelter to gain some experience. My ambition was to work with exotic captive animals, but when the Kennel Manager, Tiffany (still friends to this day) offered me a job as a kennel hand, I said yes.

While working at the shelter, I dedicated my time to learning more. I studied Animal Studies Cert II at TAFE. After working at the shelter for some time, I studied through the National Dog Trainers Federation (NDTF) in Dog Behaviour & Training Certificate III & Statement of Attainment of Dog Training Cert IV. During that time, I worked at a boarding kennel/ training centre, doggie daycare, and as a part-time trainer at another training centre.

After gaining this valuable experience over a few years, I took the leap and started my own dog training business at the end of 2011 called Nooch's Pooches Dog Behaviour & Training. Since then, I have worked with over 2000 dogs and their owners, focusing on obedience training, puppy development & behaviour modification.

Today, I host the 'Life With Your Dog' podcast, which focuses on dog training concepts and practical ideas to enrich your life with your dog. Education is the key to thriving with your dog whether you're an owner, dog trainer or enthusiast.

I train dogs for a living, but I continue to learn by attending seminars, joining think tanks, and networking with other excellent trainers worldwide to keep my skills sharp and mind open to grow as a trainer.

With the experience and knowledge that I have gained over the years, I endeavour to deliver the highest quality information, theory, and practical application in a way that can be understood and executed by everyday dog owners. This is much more than dog training; it's knowing the whys behind every command and skill so they can be executed properly. As with anything, over time as new ideas and techniques come to light, best practices can change. I recommend that you use the information in this book to build a strong training foundation but be open to continuing to learn as information is updated.

Working with dogs put me on a path to self-discovery—all credit to our beautiful dogs with whom I share my life. I hope you find value in my work and create the best life possible with your dog.

My philosophy

I believe that as humans, we have the potential to affect our immediate environment. At the very least, we can learn from what happens to us as life is our teacher, our guru.

Rocky started my journey in the dog world when he came

into my life when I was 18 years old. He was a red Kelpie and was the most intelligent dog I had ever come across. Rocky was the first dog we ever owned, and my parents got him for me while I was on an overseas holiday. When I entered the house, he ran up and gazed at me. Honestly, I felt Rocky knew who I was. This was an encounter I had never experienced before with a dog.

Rocky and I became best friends. He was always around, from when I was home sleeping, to out and about hanging with friends. He inspired me to change my bad habits and attitude to life, to transform my perspective on living in the present with things like exercising, discipline, responsibility, compassion, and most importantly, my spiritual connection.

Less than a year before acquiring Rocky, when I was 17 years old, I was brutely attacked and stabbed. It was a dark time for me, and the trauma affected certain parts of my inner world and my trust for the outside world. I was fortunate to have supportive friends and a loving family that provided me with a solid foundation in my life. However, the fear, nightmares, and anxiety still occurred daily. As mentioned, I had a good life, yet my attitude, behaviour, and some of my social network needed to change.

In hindsight, the horrific experience of being attacked was paradoxically the worst and best experience of my life, as it was the catalyst to change, growth, and resilience. Rocky certainly influenced my healing and development from a boy into a man, which eventually led to gratitude and purpose.

I would have dreams of Rocky only to wake up and find him staring straight at me. This connection with Rocky made me realise the importance of my surroundings. Through his unconditional love, he helped me become aware of myself and my journey in life. Rocky was diagnosed with leukemia at one and a half and died two weeks later. It was a very depressing time for me to have lost such a close friend. When I thought about it more, I felt he was a soul mate from the spirit world to help guide me in the right direction. With this loss came more pain to my heart than being attacked. However, it set a new awareness of my path ahead.

The message he passed on through his life was a short yet very powerful one that sparked a light inside, which started my journey of working with dogs and their beloved humans. Some time passed, and I decided to quit my job and building studies to pursue a career in the animal world. I went on a journey to find what I was destined to do with my life. It was Rocky and life herself that allowed me to see that the creator was not testing me but was showing me opportunities to practice who I wanted to become—this time of my life opened many doors to what was to come.

A couple of years passed, and in 2011, I started my own business, Nooch's Pooches, to help educate people about the connection between humans and dogs. But most importantly, it has created an inner journey connecting the mind, body, heart, and spirit.

Dogs are like four-legged mirrors. They reflect the attitudes, moods, and energy of their master and their environment. The unique thing about dogs is that they live in the NOW; they are very present, and we learn a lot about ourselves. When we create structure and routine with our dogs, with a mix of being in the right mood, using appropriate training techniques, and sharing the right state of mind, we start to see tremendous changes in how they act and see the world.

As dog owners, we must strive to be balanced to have a balanced dog. Finding this balance is different for everyone. We want to find balance physically, mentally, emotionally, and spiritually, to be aware of what is happening within and around us, and to understand how to act with good intentions. Connecting with your inner world will help you be calm, clear, and assertive in times of panic, stress, and frustration.

The book you're about to read is more than dog training. You will learn how to understand and communicate with your dog and discover a lot about yourself in the process!

The medicine our dogs bring to our lives is priceless, as the excitement they share around us and the fact that they truly live in the present moment and don't ponder on the past or future like us. We can learn so much if we pay close attention. We also know that if we enrich our dogs mentally and physically to be fulfilled, then so are we. When it comes to living with your dog, a significant part of their behaviour is determined by their environment. Biological fulfilment is necessary to thrive in life.

I have learned so much working with dogs and their owners, and I have implemented many techniques that are the same as what I teach my clients and their dogs in my own life. To have structure, move my body regularly, meditation, mind-body connection, the importance of socialisation, discipline, mindfulness, and gratitude for everything in my life, especially the small stuff. This is what I bring to my life all because dogs have changed my life and perspective for the better, and it is my opportunity to share my experiences with others.

Reflection time:

- What is it about dogs that you love so much?

- Can you find and express the same aspect in your own life?

- Why do you have a dog?

- What has your dog taught you?

- We get dogs to complement our life, not to complicate it. Have you found a way to develop, grow, learn, and love so that you can fulfil your responsibility to your dog?

- Has owning a dog made you a better person?

These are questions for you to meditate on to gain inner awareness of the mechanisms of your relationship with your dog and, ultimately, your relationship with yourself.

Most people fall in love with the story of having a dog, needing to understand the work involved to have a desirable companion. We must honour what is involved and not treat our dogs as disposable objects, they are a sacred part of our life and must be respected in all ways. Dogs have come to help humankind in traditional methods such as working for survival, hunting, agriculture, and many other forms of work and purpose. However, they also have helped us on an emotional and spiritual level that cannot be explained, only experienced.

My goal is to train people to train their dogs, to show people that the training journey is like establishing a way of life with your dog. You'll see that if you want to succeed in your training, all areas of your dog's life must be considered, managed, and maintained.

My passion is exploring what people have yet to learn from their dogs and how nature teaches us about ourselves daily while enriching our lives. My mission is to educate dog owners to find a way to offer overall biological fulfilment, structure, and activities to achieve a harmonious life between you and your dog. Developing a strong connection and communication with your dog provides a fulfilling relationship and lifelong benefits.

Using this and applying it to our lives by understanding the fundamentals of behavioural theory, science, and mind-body fulfilment can significantly enrich our lives beyond dog training. We see the positive effects of a life of discipline and structure as it is the cornerstones to happiness, health, and strength.

To be an effective leader, one must strive to be balanced in all ways, to be grounded but ambitious, courageous yet humble, intelligent and practical, compassionate and logical, and most importantly, firm yet always fair. Responsibility is what gives our life meaning, something to live for and something to struggle against. If we have this level of purpose in our lives, we may be able to make sense of all the inevitable adversities that come our way. Just like giving your dog a job gives them purpose and a way in which we relate and engage with the world, so it is true for us.

I hope you find this book and its contents to be a beneficial and practical guide to living your best life with your dog. There is so much more to cover as this beautiful rabbit hole is quite deep. On that note, this is all about establishing a solid foundation for your dog training journey.

I wish you and your dog all the best with learning, training, and a way of life to come.

About this book

Dog training is about developing a language between humans and dogs to help build the most effective and efficient way to communicate. Training your dog is also about engaging in activities that fulfil their biological needs (mind & body) which creates a lifestyle and culture balance for you and your dog to live by.

This book is to guide, educate, and provide theory to help you create a foundation to complement your training. This is not a 'quick fix' to your dog's behaviour problems. There are many variations in techniques, methods, ideologies, philosophies, and applications to training. This book provides simplified and easy-to-digest information while still diving deep into dog behaviour and training. This is my secret to success in dog training which I teach owners daily.

I wish to give you the tools that your dog needs to help minimise or eliminate behaviour issues while giving your dog the ability to live their best life!

Communication is one of the essential ingredients to a healthy relationship with your dog and the key to successful training. In this book, I'll show you that commands involve more than merely teaching your dog 'tricks'. It's about understanding what our dogs communicate to us through their body language and behaviour and how we should respond or interact with them daily.

The content of this book is focused on advice for a dog over the age of 6 months. Although I share a small section in this book on puppy training and some of the general advice in this book can work for puppies, most of the techniques, tools, and expectations are tailored for older dogs.

Using a balanced approach to training will help reinforce wanted behaviours whilst eliminating unwanted ones. I will cover information to help you understand and strengthen the practical side of your training.

My mission- EST 2011

https://me-qr.com/KS3ip90q

1
What it Means to Train Your Dog

Since the time of hunter-gatherers, humans have used dogs to fulfil specific jobs. The once wild wolf/canid integrated into communities where they worked to fulfil farming and hunting needs. Dogs could herd, hunt, retrieve, point, pull sleds, protect livestock and so much more.

Now, dogs live as companion animals, which means they miss out on having a job and purpose to follow. Dogs need to be stimulated in their minds and bodies to be fulfilled.

For example, when a dog herds, their mind is engaged with both the sheep and farmer/handler; its body backs up what the mind is saying, and it then chases and herds the sheep. Similarly, walking your dog is a physical and mental activity. They are connecting with you, their environment, and physical activity. When you return, your dog should be tired, calm, fulfilled, and happy, which works for both ends of the leash.

Every breed has different genetics, instinctive goals, and drives, but the same theory applies—all dogs need mental and physical stimulation. It is a theory that must be applied to every dog regardless of breed, temperament, energy level, and physical abilities.

The most practical 'domestic job' we can give our dogs

are loose lead walks and basic obedience training. Each complements the other, and it must be a regular activity for your dog's mind and body to benefit. Once you start to practice this daily, a remarkable thing occurs. Instead of your dog becoming overly excited when he sees the lead, he or she will understand that it's time to work and behave accordingly. This will positively impact the training and walking.

If you follow set procedures, your dog will develop focus, controlled excitement, and drive. Walking and training will become easier as your dog begins to listen, learn, and follow. Training and technique must be practical. If you overcomplicate it, your dog will be confused and frustrated while the activity ceases to be fun and engaging. Once basic obedience has been implemented into your dog's daily life, working on extra training, such as tricks or sports training, can be used to keep training dynamic, exciting, and fulfilling.

What does training your dog mean?

Throughout this book, you will learn a wide range of techniques and tips on how to manage your dog and live in harmony with your environment. You will also learn to teach your dog skills, commands, manners, and appropriate ways of living with you.

Consistency is the most important thing to remember. Your habits will become your dog's habits. Aim to develop good habits for lifelong benefits. Repetition of activities, routines, and experiences will allow your dog to learn and see the patterns. Creating a structure of rules and goals and sticking to them will be the foundation you need to communicate effectively with your dog.

Think of training as developing a language you share with your dog, a way in which understanding goes both ways. I'll teach you how dogs learn, what training is appropriate to you and your dog's level and how to work together as you guide your dog through strong leadership.

Practice skills when you don't need them to prepare you for real life when you do. One example is calling your dog to come. Think of soccer training, music practice or self-defence; training drills are often practised to be practical and functional under pressure, also called 'muscle memory'. Similar to learning a language or going to school, it is a time to learn how to communicate and form relationships with others.

Training should also be like a game of sport or exercise that challenges the body while stimulating the mind. Your dog will learn the art of discipline while playing 'games' that are fun, exciting, and challenging. Dogs and owners benefit from the health benefits of being active as well as optimal fulfilment and relationship building.

Obedience training ticks three boxes:

- Teaching practical, functional skills

- Mental stimulation

- Relationship building between owner and dog

The more this is practised regularly, the more the

communication with your dog improves. Trust will grow as you maintain healthy communication and management of your dog.

I've learned over the last decade that the best dog trainers I know manage their dogs and training very carefully. Setting your dog up for success is essential, remembering that dogs are usually trying to better their situation to serve their desires. It is up to us as owners and trainers to prepare our dogs early (especially in the first 18 months) to understand being rewarded for good behaviour, corrected for unwanted behaviour, or removed from an undesirable situation when necessary. Having the right equipment, mindset, technique, and approach is what you will learn throughout this book.

2

Understanding the Theory of Dog Behaviour

Dog body language

To be successful in understanding what your dog is experiencing and to be able to communicate with your dog, it is essential that you know basic dog body language. Since dogs cannot speak, it is up to us as owners, handlers, and trainers to be aware of what our dogs are feeling and communicating through their body language in every situation and environment.

Take the time to know when your dog is excited, scared, stressed, and in what state of drive—aggressive, anxious, or relaxed, etc. Once you start to understand when your dog is in a particular state, this becomes the beginning of modifying your dog's behaviour to suit your training plan and, essentially, your lifestyle. Being proactive in this approach rather than reactive is the best way to achieve your goals in training.

For example, suppose you are walking your dog and are in the process of eliminating barking at other people. In that case, your best proactive approach is to know when your dog is about to bark by assessing their body language. If you try to stop your dog's barking by waiting for them to bark, this is reactive, and it can be hard to change their mind. Furthermore, we see barking as the problem behaviour, but the best way to fix a problem is to identify its cause. Is the dog barking out of excitement, frustration, or fear? The way to determine and identify the cause of the barking is by reading body language, the context of the environment, and many other variables at play.

As humans, we generally depend on speaking as our preferred communication method. However, we must remind ourselves that 60% of our communication with other humans is through body language. If your friend tells you they are okay while their body language clearly says the opposite, you know something is wrong. Reading your dog's body language is essential because most people spend too much time talking to their dogs (with words that do not mean anything to the dog), expecting their dog to understand them. Dogs hear sounds, not words. It has been said that dogs are prewired from birth to read our body language and recognise threats to the friendly body language of humans without having to learn or experience it.

When learning canine body language, it is best to be aware of the dog's whole body, from the ears, tail, eyes, posture, mouth, etc. Below are images of classic dog body language to better understand this.

It is safe to say that most owners are aware of a happy dog by its wagging tail. However, the context of the situation and breed can make this an incomplete observation. Generally, a happy dog's tail wags in a figure 8 style (side to side), whereas a dog that is alert, aroused or threatened can have a stiff high tail, which is called 'flagging', which may be confused with a 'happy wagging tail'. This is why being aware of your dog's body gestures is critical.

Another example of misunderstanding body language can be when looking at dogs of the Spitz breeds (Husky, Pomeranian, Malamute, Japanese Spitz, Akita, etc.) because their tails are generally always curled up due to their breed specification. Their coat can make it hard to see changes in their body (e.g. if hackles are up).

There are exceptions to these rules, so it is up to you to study and get to know your dog. Know the guidelines and apply them when making your observations This will help you to be aware of what your dog is expressing to others and the world around them.

Another good practice is being in tune with your body language and gestures when you are interacting and training your dog. They are master observers and study your every movement. Since dogs are visually orientated and learn via body language and patterns of behaviour/environmental stimulus, they know when things are about to happen by the patterns of movement we project to them. They can also read our micro expressions (voluntary and involuntary emotional responses), which can affect your communication with your dog positively or negatively.

Throughout this book, we will explore many concepts of how dogs learn, and you will also learn through your training how important your gestures are in shaping behaviour. It is easy to shape commands and behaviour using physical gestures. It is more advanced when your dog only follows verbal commands. Stay in tune with what you tell your dog through your habits, patterns, and gestures. Know that you cannot lie to your dog. They know when you are happy, excited, distracted, and frustrated.

If you can read your dog's patterns effectively, you can intervene, manage, or use training techniques to modify your dog's behaviour with less stress, better communication, and guidance. Be aware of your dog's behaviour patterns and body language. Don't compare your dog to how other dogs behave. Compare your dog to how they acted in a previous situation/same context.

Body language is essential to understanding behaviour and training, but practising and being mindful of what is occurring within your dog's environment is crucial. For example, if I see my dog's tail curl up, I look around to see what my dog is looking at or focused on. On the other hand, if I see a dog in the distance approaching, I look at my dog to see what they feel about that by assessing their body language.

Body language and the environment go hand in hand. Developing this awareness of your dog's behaviour patterns is a necessary skill. Once you understand canine body language, it will be easier for you to assess how you are progressing in training and behaviour modification and what the next steps should be.

Sometimes signals are subtle so knowing how your dog communicates its needs is the key to your success.

Take a close look at the illustrations that follow and watch your dog closely for these behaviours.

Body language signal summary

Relaxed Posture: Your dog will have a loose stance with the head high. Ears will be up and relaxed, but not forward. Eyes will be open and the tail down and relaxed. The mouth will open slightly with the tongue exposed. (Happy Face)

Alert: Your dog will lean slightly forward, and the ears may twitch to catch a sound. Eyes will be wide open, and the tail will be horizontal and may move from side to side. The mouth will be closed.

Threatening/ Dominant/Aggression: Posture will be up, forward still/stiff and piloerect (Hackles raised). Ears will be pushed forward and the eyes glaring, large and round. The tail will be stiff, high and flagging side to side. The mouth will be short with the teeth exposed and lips curled.

Fear Aggressive: The body and head will be lowered, piloerection (Hackles). The ears will be back and flat, and the eyes round with dilated pupils. The tail will be tucked and lowered. The mouth will be open and teeth exposed.

Fear Submissive/ Appeasement: The body and head will be lowered and sometimes a paw raised. The ears will be back and flat with the eyes small, elongated and blinking. The tail will be tucked and lowered, while the mouth will be long with no teeth and lip licking.

Stress/ Anxiety: The body and head will be lowered and the ears back and flat. The eyes will be small, elongated and constantly looking around. The tail will be tucked and lowered and the mouth will be panting rapidly.

Appeasement/ Fear/ Total Submission: The dog will roll onto its back, exposing its vital areas. The ears will be back and flat and the eyes will be partly closed with an averted gaze. The tail will be between the legs with the mouth closed.

Play Bow: The dog will bow with the front end lowered. The ears will be up and pupils dilated. The tail will be up and wag from side to side like a figure eight, and the mouth will be open with the tongue out.

Classical/Pavlovian conditioning

Pavlovian (Classical) conditioning is a learning process that occurs when two stimuli are repeatedly paired: a response that is at first elicited by the second stimulus is eventually elicited by the first stimulus alone.

Ivan Pavlov was a Russian psychologist in the early 1900s studying a dog's digestive system. He had a tube connecting to the dog's mouth and another tube connecting to the salivation glands to test how much the dog would salivate when eating. Pavlov introduced a bell to signal that the food was about to be fed through the tubes. Every time the bell would ring, the dog would receive food from the tube. This experiment repeated over time, and one day, the food paste machine stopped working; immediately as the bell rang, the dog started to salivate as if the food was presented to him.

These findings surprised Pavlov, and he started to understand that when a stimulus (the bell) is repeated and consistently provided, an action (the food), a specific association/ emotion called a conditioned response, is created (salivation).

Classical conditioning occurs to us humans when we hear a song. It triggers an emotion of 'the good old days', and you get goosebumps, or when you smell a perfume that reminds you of a particular person or hear the same ringtone as your own, you will reflexively reach for your phone. These are subconscious responses to a stimulus that elicits emotion and behaviour.

This form of conditioning is used throughout the dog training experience. Now that you know this, start to pay more attention to your dog's behaviour in response to conditioned stimuli, such as your dog's reaction to the doorbell ringing, picking up your keys, picking up the leash, and saying certain words. These actions may trigger your dog's behaviour because of their association.

Operant/Instrumental conditioning

Operant/ Instrumental conditioning is a learning process in which behaviour is modified by its consequence's reinforcing or punishing effect.

This form of conditioning is more direct and initiates understanding that there are consequences to behaviours performed. In instrumental conditioning, reinforcement or punishment increases or decreases the probability that a behaviour will occur again—e.g., if you pat your dog for jumping up on you, they learn that jumping will produce that reinforcement which means your dog will jump on you more frequently and sometimes more intensely. Behaviour creates the outcome.

IMPORTANT: Dogs can only connect behaviour and its consequence within 1.6 seconds!

This form of conditioning was founded by BF Skinner when he discovered that rats learned to press a button to receive a food reward. Operant conditioning is a necessary and the most straightforward form of conditioning for us to integrate and apply in training compared to the conscious application of classical conditioning. Knowing both and how to fuse both forms of conditioning is where science and art meet. These conditioning processes occur every time your dog experiences the world and cannot be eliminated, which means you are training your dog every time you are together, knowingly, or unknowingly.

Matrix of motivation

There are many ways to motivate your dog to perform behaviours and learn new skills. The table below, called the matrix of motivation, shows various elements that outline what makes us do or not do certain things. This is relatable to our dog training and our own life.

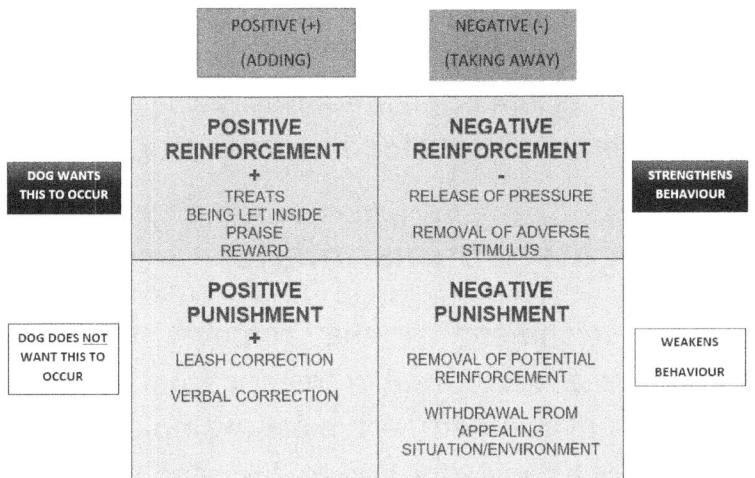

Use of positive reinforcement

Positive reinforcement is a common phrase used in behaviour modification because it adds something desirable to your dog that strengthens behaviour for future repetition.

Giving food to a hungry dog that performed a behaviour you find desirable is the classic example of positive reinforcement but, indeed, not the only form. Rewarding your dog with food, pats, praise, balls, or tugs is a common form of positive reinforcement.

Use of negative reinforcement

Negative reinforcement is the removal or ceasing of an adverse stimulus that, when removed, the dog finds reinforcing. A typical example of negative reinforcement is when you apply leash pressure on the dog's collar to communicate that the behaviour displayed when removing leash pressure is desirable—e.g., when telling a dog to 'SIT', upward pressure on the dog's collar is uncomfortable, and the moment your dog lowers their butt on the ground is the moment the pressure is released. This is where the dog has been negatively reinforced for their behaviour.

Use of negative punishment

Negative punishment is the removal of potential reinforcement or withdrawal of the dog from an appealing situation or environment. A typical example of negative punishment is asking your dog to 'SIT', and if they refuse to follow the command, you withhold the food they are expecting. Another example is if your dog is inside your home performing undesirable behaviour, such as jumping on the couch. Removing your dog from inside the house and taking them outside is a form of negative punishment.

Remember the 'matrix of motivation', the word negative

is mathematical/scientific, referring to the removal or withdrawal of something, not negative to be emotional (bad/wrong). It's important to realise that your dog is likely doing something to gain access to a potential reinforcement, and removing that potential is punishing to the dog. When your dog is barking at the back door as you approach the door to let them in, simply turning around and walking away can be a form of negative punishment, taking away the potential of you opening the door and letting your dog enter.

Use of positive punishment

Positive punishment is the addition/ application of something undesirable to weaken behaviour for future scenarios. A leash pop — applying a short sharp correction on the leash—when your dog is on a leash and jumps on somebody, is considered positive punishment. Your dog will find your response aversive, weakening the behaviour in the future.

If you decide to use positive punishment, it has to be absolutely clear to the dog why the consequence has taken place. Punishment is used when you want to create an aversive effect to the behaviour you never want to occur again (e.g., jumping on people) or in some circumstances it's applied when your dog knows the command and chooses to ignore the command. There are many nuances to this which I will discuss throughout this book. Still, it is limited and usually best learnt from a trained professional and with the correct intention and attitude by the handler.

Note: Punishment should not be issued from an

emotional state. You need to remain calm and create an association between the positive punishment and undesirable behaviour, while not letting out your frustration or anger.

Stimulus definition

A stimulus is an external input (sound, event, or thing) that holds a particular value or consequence to an individual. For example, if your dog is reactive to other dogs, then the other dog is the stimulus. If your dog is bothered by thunder, then thunder is the stimulus. Your verbal command is also a stimulus. Anything outside of your dog that your dog recognises is a stimulus, and utilising this language helps remove emotion from the behaviour modification process.

The three elements of puppy training and development

Raising a puppy can be stressful yet fulfilling as you develop a relationship with your pup and set them up for their life journey. Puppy development is an in-depth topic that needs its own book, but the foundational elements of puppy training (six months and younger) are a great place to start. As we move through the dog training process, it will become obvious that training a dog older than six months significantly differs from training and raising a young puppy, as techniques, tools, and expectations vary.

My puppy development programs set up a puppy for a successful life. In this section, I'll cover the three main elements of puppy training and development that offer some perspective on developing the foundations of your puppy's life.

1. Critical period of development

2. Management in/out of your home

3. Teaching your puppy how to learn

Critical period of development

The critical period of a puppy's psychological development is 7-17 weeks. This means that what your puppy is exposed to during this time is what they build most of their experiences from. Your aim should be to get your pup out and about as early as you get them.

Start slowly by getting your puppy used to wearing a harness and a lead. Walk around the house and reward with high-value treats when your pup is focused on you and walking around. Some puppies will be unsure about wearing something wrapped on their body, but time and using your treats to help them focus on you will get them used to it.

Your first walk will only consist of walking in the driveway or front yard where you live. Remember, you need your treats! Reward when your pup is looking in your direction or while exploring. If your puppy is scared, be patient and take things slow. Don't force them.

As the days go on, walk along the footpath and stroll locally, exposing your pup to everything around, like cars, people, other dogs, animals, and the sounds of the surrounding environment. The most crucial part of what you will learn in my puppy training is that building your dog's confidence and socialisation is something you can't get back later in life.

The confusion is when your vet advises that your pup stays inside your property until they are fully vaccinated, which can be up to 15-17 weeks old. This is very late in the critical period. Your vet has the same intention as we do, to have a happy, healthy, and social puppy that will develop to live a fulfilled life, so this advice can be confusing.

The viruses and diseases your pup can contract are genuine and potentially life-threatening. However, many suburban areas (like Sydney, Australia) have a very high rate of owners who own vaccinated dogs. The number of pups contracting these illnesses is dramatically lower than before vaccination protocols, which are a regular practice. So your area should be considered when making an informed decision.

Since 2011, when I started Nooch's Pooches, I have given the same advice to every puppy owner I see, and I have not had one reported incident of any issues of a puppy getting sick. The real problem is the parvovirus which can live in the soil for up to a year. Contamination can occur if an infected dog poops in that spot, and if your pup comes into direct contact with the virus, it can contract it. The risk is up to you.

However, I genuinely believe more dogs die (behavioural euthanasia) due to their behaviour (fear aggression) because of a lack of socialisation from early puppyhood, than dying of parvovirus—in the areas that have not had an outbreak or high cases of parvo or other diseases reported—in that area.

A lack of habituation and socialisation to the world you

want your puppy to live in can most likely develop fear and insecurity, which results in aggression, anxiety, anti-social behaviour and timidity. Be proactive and ensure you don't create a problem that can be hard to fix later in your dog's life.

The guidelines and rules to follow when walking your young puppy before final immunisation include:

- Stay away from dog parks and highly dog-populated areas.
- Try to keep off the grass.
- Avoid poop smelling.
- Interact with vaccinated dogs only.
- Always keep your pup on a leash.

Management for puppies in and outside of the home

Puppies are generally too young to understand appropriate and inappropriate behaviours, especially when young, so you must set your pup up for success. They do not understand our expectations and are learning what we want from them; you must micro-manage every interaction and experience they have by puppy-proofing your home and properly controlling how they experience the outside world.

Inside your home, you must have an appropriate area to set up a crate and exercise pen and secure your backyard, balcony, and courtyard to ensure your puppy is safe and contained.

A puppy under the age of six months should wear a harness when out and about. Do not attach a leash to your puppy's collar when walking out of your house for a few main reasons:

- Safety: They could slip out of the collar. Use a firmly fitted harness (H style harness), not a 'step in' harness, as they can slip out of these harnesses quite easily.

Trachea damage: Pulling on a collar can cause damage to a growing puppy's trachea. Puppies will not understand how to manage pressure on the collar for loose lead walking as they are too young to understand the consequences in a highly stimulating environment. I teach dogs over six months old how to lose lead walk and understand the pressure on the collar for obedience-type training.

- Desensitisation: Walking a pup on a collar and allowing them to pull into it for the duration of their walk will desensitise them to pressure on their collar, which may affect collar training when they are ready for a training collar.

You want to ensure that you build a puppy's confidence when experiencing the world, and the best way to do this is to provide a positive or neutral experience with external stimuli. If you fail to manage your pup appropriately, such as not using the correct equipment or granting them too much freedom too soon, you risk creating an adverse situation and experience for them that may affect the rest of their life.

A simple example is if you let your puppy run free in the park and they choose to run up to another dog. This may create an adverse effect as the other dog may not be social and attack or jump on your pup. An acute adverse situation that your puppy experiences (single event learning), especially in their critical period, may create a fear response that's difficult to overcome. In this example, the single event could negatively affect your puppy's socialisation with other dogs.

Remember that in the early months of your puppy's life, they are learning all about the world around them. It is up to you to set up each situation to keep your pup safe and help it learn how to behave in each different environment by following these actions:

- Set your pup up for successful house training by having an exercise pen and crate to keep them inside when unsupervised, otherwise your puppy may learn to eliminate (pee or poop) anywhere they wish or to destroy furniture and other items in the house.

- If you give your puppy too much freedom inside and outside your house, you may develop the wrong behaviours you don't wish to see as they age.

- If your pup learns to run away from you when you're out of the house and doesn't see you as the most valuable thing in their world, you have failed in your management strategies. Using a leash, long-lead, crate and puppy-proofing are all part of good management.

Manage your pup, set them up for success, and keep them safe. Over time you will be able to grant them more freedom.

However, you must remember that they are too young to know what is best for themselves, and if you wish to get the most out of your training, you must first make them confident before teaching them manners.

Teaching your puppy how to learn

In the first six months of your puppy's life, you are teaching them how to learn and develop a solid foundation through participating in fun games that will benefit your overall obedience training strategy. Your expectations for your puppy when teaching the basic commands is that your pup learns skills, and more importantly, how to earn rewards from you.

You can successfully teach some basic commands at this early age. Doing this can significantly improve your training journey by helping your dog move through the training system more effectively when they are older. You want training to be like learning a language. There are no corrections for getting the commands wrong; however, you can withhold rewards if they are not displaying the desirable behaviour. Be patient and enjoy the process.

Once you make training a fun activity, and they start to display competence in it, you can enter the 'training phase' of each behaviour. You have to teach a pup how to follow and learn from you to make it easier to advance in the later stages of their development.

If you begin to put too much pressure on your puppy too early, you risk making training a daunting activity and may crush their spirit. You want to build their confidence and competence before using pressure to make them do what you want, especially for puppies 4-5 months old. Although they are showing more interest and competence, they are still too young to make them follow your commands, so keep it super fun and positive.

When it comes to raising, training, and developing your puppy, you must consider these three elements in your daily schedule and routine to set a puppy up for the years of training and experiences you will encounter. If you follow these points, and work with the right trainer, you will be in the position to set your pup up for success in all areas of life. By establishing an effective system early, you will be able to successfully implement the content of this book into your training plan and life with your dog.

Importance of play for dogs

Dogs are social creatures. They rely on social order and cooperation amongst the pack/family, which is necessary for the them to thrive. Play is an essential time of a dog's life; it is a time to strengthen bonds, enrich them mentally and establish order within the family or pack.

Like humans, socialisation through play usually happens with people they know, like, and respect, giving their lives meaning and kinship. Humans find many ways to play, such as games, sports, dance, and sharing like-minded experiences.

Play comes in many forms for dogs as well through their training. Providing play for your dog is necessary for optimal fulfillment.

Types of play for your dog:

- Ball play

- Tug play

- Rough house play (wrestle-type play)

- Playing food games

- Play with other dogs

Your dog's temperament, breed, age, and gender will determine their appropriate play style. It is most beneficial to find a play style that you and your dog are involved in (two-player games). Games like tug or ball are good choices if your dog finds them reinforcing or simply training daily with food. Scheduling time for hands-on play with your dog is not only good for training but also a time to engage and have fun together.

Developing your relationship with your dog is one of the essential foundations to successful training. Utilising play as a reward for behaviours and access to that play is fundamental to the outcome of your training. Once you've built a strong bond with your furry friend, they will not only obey your commands and behave well because they want to avoid punishment, but they'll genuinely want to follow you as a respected leader. This happens not through coercion but through cooperation and understanding. It's beautiful when you and your dog can work together as a team!

Your dog playing with other dogs that you know is also beneficial, especially when your dog is young. Dogs that live together or dogs of friends/family you see regularly, if appropriate, can benefit from playtime with each other. The play must be mutual, and all dogs should play within acceptable boundaries.

Allowing your dog to play with all dogs, all the time, is not the best habit to form for many reasons. If play is an essential time in your dog's life, why outsource that time to random dogs? We must see random dogs as just random dogs and not as an opportunity for play. Since playing is a part of training, it's important to maintain control over who they play with and when. Remember that socialisation doesn't always mean playing. It also means being calm and comfortable in the presence of other dogs. Play can be acceptable in socialisation but must be at the right time and place.

This does not mean that my dogs do not play with random dogs because they do; however, the play that comes from me is more engaging, and reliable than the play they get from others. For example, at the end of my training sessions, I encourage my dog Chilli, when appropriate, to play with a dog he doesn't know, like a client's dog. During that playtime, I still use my commands to show him that a better form of play will come from me.

The problem with a dog park setting is that letting your dog run free with random dogs can be dangerous. Your dog gets attacked or bitten by another dog, resulting in fear-based behaviours (aggression, timidity, and reactivity), or it's where your dog learns to ignore you and view other random dogs as more exciting and fun. Both of these outcomes can damage your training, so beware of the consequences of allowing your dog to create experiences outside of the parameters you've set for their well-being and development.

Think about how you incorporate play into your own life. Is it with random people always, or is it with a consistent group or individuals? If you participate in play with others, how does that affect your relationship with them?

Your dog relies on you for the bare necessities. Play may seem like an optional chore and easier to outsource to other dogs, but the reward you get back by creating regular playtime with them is priceless, especially when it comes to developing a valuable relationship.

Playing TUG- Tips for play

https://me-qr.com/TZe6q9jv

Distress vs. eustress

There are two types of stress—distress and eustress. 'Distress' refers to stresses that cause an undesirable state, whereas 'eustress' refers to positive stresses through which growth occurs.

The common misconception is that all stress is bad. However, you can only attain the growth of a new skill by experiencing some level of stress in the mind and body.

The best example can be when applying this understanding to bodybuilding. You cannot grow muscle without putting a load of stress on the body, which creates micro-tears within the muscle. The repair of the muscle is what is responsible for growth and strength. A similar concept goes for the mind, learning new things can be stressful and frustrating. Overcoming the frustration and achieving success in solving the equation or coming to the point of understanding a concept brings on the development of new and improved skill acquisition.

Too much stress that cannot be overcome can lead to distress, hindering the learning process. Stress affects learning in positive and negative ways. When teaching and training your dog, it's important for you to know your dog's limits, temperament and behaviour, and to understand what your dog can endure in any situation. You also must learn how to give your dog the illusion of control during training sessions to help them avoid and escape stressful consequences so you can modify their behaviour.

Developing impulse control is a stressful process. When executed correctly, it falls under the eustress category. While your dog is under the influence of a high-drive state of mind, aroused and in pursuit of a particular item, it can be very frustrating to command your dog to perform a specific behaviour opposite to the impulse to pursue a stimulus. Playing tug can be a great example. All your dog wants to do is jump and bite the tug.

Throughout a training session, it's important to teach and train your dog to perform obedience commands to earn the game of tug. At first, this can be stressful and frustrating;

however, once your dog successfully obtains the reward, it becomes a new skill that can be applied in other areas of life.

Do not shy away from stressful situations, and certainly avoid your dog experiencing distress whenever possible. Still, small doses of eustress are necessary and help promote learning, especially when applying training to everyday life. Know your dog and guide them through these experiences to become a more robust and more intelligent version of themselves.

3

The Fundamentals: Building the Foundations

What you will need

It's important to the success of any training program to consistently use the appropriate equipment and tools for your dog. Most of the equipment I suggest is for both safety and training potential. For example, using the the correct collar will help you prevent your dog from slipping out of the collar and also help with loose lead walking and better control over your dog. Remember that equipment and tools alone do not fix problems, but using them with proper technique and application make training more successful.

I have made plenty of mistakes over the years, so I hope you can learn from my experience and not repeat mistakes I've made and witnessed along the way.

Also, understand that the practicality of specific equipment may not seem necessary at the beginning of our training program but will come into effect later, so develop good habits from the start.

Things you will need:

- **Flat leash:** Be mindful of the design, ensuring it is

safe by having a good-sized buckle and is practical to work with. Nylon or leather is my preference. For large and powerful dogs, purchase a strong leash to handle the load and avoid cheap leads! Some cheap leads are glued under the plastic cover so are not as strong as they seem.

- **Slip lead:** All dogs are to be introduced to a slip lead for walking and training.

- **Martingale collar:** Some dogs over six months are fitted with this collar as their main training and walking collar. The martingale collar is used for all dogs that are attached to a long leash. Below, I will show you how this collar fits appropriately for best results.

- **Treat pouch:** Used for quick access to reward your dog in a timely manner and keep things clean. No food in pockets, zip lock bags or bum bags as it makes training more complicated, especially in the early stages of your training.

- **High-value food:** Something your dog loves and is soft so it doesn't crumble and swallows quickly, or daily rations of your dog's food.

- **10 m leash:** For a fun time in the park to sniff, pee, poop, chase the ball, train, etc., while still allowing you to control.

- **Bed:** A dog bed, blanket or mat. This will be part of teaching our dog a controlled position.

THE FUNDAMENTALS: BUILDING THE FOUNDATIONS 33

- **Ball or tug:** Something of a very high value that will be used as a reward for your dog if your dog has the drive and desire to chase a ball or tug.

- **Crate:** Metal crate that is strong enough for your dog not to escape out of it. It is large enough that your dog can stand and turn a full circle in it. Avoid cheap metal crates or material crates as they can be a danger to your dog's safety and your training.

Slip leash

The slip leash is one of the most essential tools in my dog training programs.

It is important to know the type of material, dimensions, and most of all, how to fit and use it. I prefer a particular slip leash that is 6 mm, polyester with nylon threading; the stopper is high-quality spring-loaded, and won't slip or fail under pressure. There are various styles, qualities and makes of slip leashes; not all are safe (fail under pressure) or useful(do not produce a reliable and desirable effect).

A slip leash must be tough enough not to break or tear under pressure while still being comfortable to hold in your hand. It also must be able to consistently release pressure immediately and effectively .

Slip leashes are universal in size, however, you need to put it on correctly for it to be a useful tool in your training. Always keep the collar high on neck, behind the ears and under the jaw.

When putting the slip leash on, make sure you can see the

'p' of the leash. 'p' for proper and 'q' for not quiet, this means when your dog is in front facing you, hold the slip leash in front of you so you can see the 'p'.

It's important to fit the slip leash on correctly, so when your dog is on your left hand side and you apply pressure and release, the slip leash should release pressure immediately. If you fit the slip leash on with the 'q', you will notice when you apply and release pressure on the leash it will not release, the tension will remain. This guideline is for when your dog is on your left hand side, and opposite if you like your dog on your right hand side.

Slip lead: How to fit them correctly

https://me-qr.com/SKoXvMPF

Introducing slip lead & leash pressure

https://me-qr.com/clAFcpUv

Martingale collar

The martingale, also known as a half check or obedience collar, is a collar that has a chain that connects via D rings to a nylon collar. The leash is attached to the ring that activates the chain to apply pressure to the collar and when pressure is removed, the collar loosens immediately.

This collar is not as strong or responsive as the slip leash; however, it is a very valuable tool. It is useful as a main walking and training collar for some dogs that are not strong-willed or strong-bodied and for smaller dogs. If a dog walks and trains on a slip leash, I tend to use the martingale as a collar attached to a long lead, so it's worth having both in your toolbox.

Keeping all training collars high on the neck when walking and training is key to gaining the best leverage and maintaining control with minimal pressure. This collar works best when you fit it correctly, ensuring the 2 D rings the chain runs through do not touch, allowing the pressure on the collar to distribute evenly along the neck. Watch the video in the QR code below for instructions.

Martingale collars are not only used for training but are a great safety tool. Fitting your martingale collar correctly is essential for training and walking, however, even if not fitted correctly (and assuming it's the correct size for your dog), your dog will not be able to slip out of this collar as the rings tighten when pressure is applied. The martingale collars I use do not have buckles, which means you need to manually adjust the size when on your dog's neck. This is beneficial as buckles tend to break at the worst times which could lead to your dog running off.

A guide to how to use a martingale collar

https://me-qr.com/fUtyOXz1

10 m long lead

The 10 m long lead is an essential tool in your dog training journey. This allows you to have control and communication with your dog when in a park or practicing recalls and commands from a distance. It also allows you to offer free time to your dog while under your control.

It is essential to ensure you have a strong long lead that will not break under tension. For larger breeds, I use a nylon, 16 mm wide, long lead with a brass buckle to ensure safety. Cheaper materials tend to snap and fail under pressure. I recommend purchasing a long lead from a reputable working or sport dog website.

Storing and wrapping a long lead for longevity is always the best practice. As soon as you see a knot in the leash, you must unknot immediately, otherwise your lead will begin to fray and rip. Also, wrapping it correctly helps with travelling back and forth to the park without the hassle of a tangled messy lead. QR codes below share some advice for wrapping and handling long leads.

How to wrap and pack away long lead

https://me-qr.com/ePNDSsIS

Long lead handling & safety tips

https://me-qr.com/PM9w7Koy

The 3 P's

The 3 P's to developing skills are practice, patience, and persistence. This is key to ensuring any training program is successful. Building foundations, obedience commands, conditioning of behaviours and their longevity are related to how the 3 P's are a part of your mindset and training attitude.

There are many reasons why people fail to reach their goals when training their dogs, and some are (but are not limited to) people who expect too much too quickly from their dogs and need to practice more consistently with what has been set out for them.

The tricky part of dog training is that if people are unwilling to change their habits and routines with their dogs, it will be difficult to see long-term changes in their dog's behaviour.

Training your dog is an art form because of many different variables. We cannot rationalise and talk things through with our dogs so they can make better decisions. They have different agendas and motivations of their own (learnt or genetic) that do not match our own, and they are a product of their environment most of the time.

Management, training routines and thinking ahead are some practices we must adopt to successfully achieve our goals with our dogs.

Practice:

- Be consistent with your training routine.
- Make it a daily ritual with your dog.
- It takes hundreds of repetitions to create reliable behaviour.
- Your dog's habits and behaviours are produced by repetition.

Patience:

- Don't expect significant changes overnight.
- Baby steps to success, not giant leaps of failure.
- If you feel frustrated with your dog, finish your

training session, and come back again later.

- Always end on a positive note.

- Just think of a giant oak tree that starts from a seed.

- Learn to acknowledge your dog's small achievements, this will help you realise how much progress you are making.

Persistence:

- If you do not feel like training your dog, then do it anyway.

- Follow through with your routines, and don't make shortcuts.

- Be consistent with your training.

- Remember, if you always do what you always did, you will always get what you always got.

- If you know your dog knows a command or a certain way to behave in a situation, ensure you do not let your dog disobey a command.

- Be reliable.

Charging the marker ('YES')

The first element of the practical side of your training is 'charging' the food marker, which will be the word 'YES'. You say the word 'YES', and within 1.6 seconds, your dog must have a treat in their mouth. As you do this over the next couple of days, you will begin to see that your dog will turn towards you, expecting a reward as soon as you say the word 'YES'.

A marker is a signal, usually an audible cue (verbal, mechanical or visual), that announces a particular consequence will follow. We use many markers in training. A marker for positive reinforcement of food is 'YES' a marker for negative punishment is 'NO', often called a non-reinforcement marker (means no reward for the behaviour performed) or a marker for positive punishment 'UH-UH' (means leash correction) and all markers are at first paired with a consequence to follow to develop the conditioned response, the association between the cue and the chosen stimulus.

The first thing I like to teach dogs is a verbal marker for positive reinforcement, 'YES'. As we have only roughly 1.6 seconds to communicate to our dogs that they have done the right thing, we must be clear about what they did for the food reward to be delivered. To charge this marker, you must say 'YES' and, within 1.6 seconds, give your dog food. Repeating this process even up to only 14 repetitions, you will notice your dog anticipates food is coming, and you'll see this by observing their body language. I usually use a different tone, pitch, and inflexion when saying 'YES'(sounds like 'ESS') to keep it a specific sound and not confuse my dogs when I'm saying this word in regular everyday life.

Creating a clear and reliable marker is super essential for a couple of reasons:

- We want the word 'YES' to specifically mean that you will reward that behaviour that was happening at that moment. It pinpoints the exact behaviour you want to reinforce with a high-value food reward.

- Dogs are masters of reading body language and picking up on gestures before understanding verbal commands. You may notice that your dog knows food is coming when you reach for your treat pouch or pocket or hear the rustle of a zip-lock bag. So, having a clear marker to announce reward is on the way is essential for reinforcing the correct behaviour with good timing, clarity, and effectiveness so that we can give a marker before reaching for food at the exact moment of the desirable behaviour.

- It bridges the word 'YES' and the treat you will give. E.g., my dog Spades was 20 m away from me in a down-stay, under a tree, while I was in the middle of a training session with my clients. A dog walked past Spades, and all he did was sniff the air, but he DID NOT break position. I thought that was amazing for his level of training, so I said 'YES' loudly so he could hear me. Spades immediately snapped his head toward me, knowing I was about to reward him. Spades waited 10 seconds for me to give him that treat while the whole time waiting with anticipation & excitement. Spades heard the word 'YES' when he noticed the dog, and I was satisfied with his behaviour.

- Even though the treat came 10 seconds later, he still knew he got rewarded when I said 'YES' and not when

I gave him the food. You will have a 10-second bridge sometime soon. However, most dogs will achieve a 5-second bridge with consistency as you advance through your obedience training over the next couple of weeks.

The marker is one of my training system's most crucial foundational components. We want to be clear, concise, and consistent with our dogs, especially when we want to reinforce behaviour to repeat in the future.

MAKE SURE YOU ONLY SAY 'YES' WHEN YOU GIVE A TREAT. Say 'good dog' for pats and praise. We want the word 'YES' to mean that your dog is rewarded with food and 'good boy' for praise. DON'T USE THE WORD 'YES' AND NOT GIVE A TREAT!

When charging the marker for FOOD, I like to use it as a durational marker which means when the dog hears 'YES', I want the dog to stay in behaviour to receive the reward, and when they hear the release command 'OK', your dog is free to come out of the position. I do this to keep the dog in a lower state of arousal (calmer and less drive), which can be more manageable for most pet owners.

In saying this, if you prefer to use 'YES' as a reward + release out of behaviour, this is still good and has great function. For the context of this book, know that the marker 'YES' means food comes to the dog, and they must stay in behaviour unless instructed otherwise.

Let me give you and your dog an example, assuming you have charged the marker correctly. You are sitting at the dinner table, and your dog typically jumps up and annoys you, hoping to get some food. You will ignore your dog while they jump up on you. As soon as they stop and relax, you say 'YES' and reward. Keep saying 'YES' and reward every time your dog shows the behaviour you like.

The marker allows you to reward a specific behaviour that your dog understands. If you do not have a marker, it can be difficult to reward a particular behaviour. The marker will allow you to tell your dog they have done the correct behaviour, and you will have time to retrieve the treat (that may be on the other side of the room), and your dog will wait for it until you give it to them. This is called a bridge.

Remember:

- Say the word 'YES'.

- Within 1.6 seconds, give your dog the treat.

- Do this randomly throughout the day/night when you are with your dog.

- Make sure you say 'YES' before you proceed to feed your dog.

- After a week of practice, you can start to space out the 'YES'and your reward by a couple of seconds.

- Once you practice this consistently over a few weeks, you can say 'YES', and your dog will know they are getting rewarded even though you give the food up to 5 seconds after the 'YES'.

- Always give a treat for 'YES' and use 'good boy/girl' for pats and praise.

Different markers

Not all dogs are only motivated by food. Many dogs prefer to chase the ball than to work or focus on the food they have. Others may choose to play a game of tug. Because of this, we need more than one 'marker' ('YES') for our dog to know exactly what reward is going to be delivered.

I prefer to teach dogs most commands with food (using luring) to establish and teach new behaviours. Once the dog knows the behaviour I am asking, I can switch to rewarding with a ball or tug (depending on what the dog is motivated by).

When a dog is chasing a ball or playing tug, they are in prey drive, which generally means the dog is in a heightened state of mind, more excited, more active, and in a chase/bite state of mind). If your dog is highly motivated by the ball or tug, we can use this to improve our training and make training more dynamic and enriching.

Play is essential, especially if your dog has prey drive; it becomes an opportunity:

- Play is a bonding experience and, with regular practice, will strengthen your bond with your dog.

- To improve impulse control, your dog must learn to do a task/follow a command to receive the reward of tug/ball. Perform passive behaviour for an active game.

- Reward your dog with what they want the most, a

more valuable reinforcer for behaviour.

- Start by making an association between a verbal cue and its action.

For the ball

You can use the word 'FETCH' (or any marker/cue you choose) and throw the ball. Repeat this over the next few days. Your next step is to give the command, e.g., 'SIT' when the dog sits, 'FETCH', + throw the ball. Practice this with the commands your dog is confident with (refer to the training or proofing phase).

For the TUG

Say 'TUG' (or any marker/cue you choose), present tug, and proceed to play. Repeat this over the next few days. Your next step is to give the command, e.g., 'SIT' when the dog sits, 'TUG', + play tug with your dog. Practice this with the commands your dog is confident with (refer to the training or proofing phase).

Using TUG as a reward

https://me-qr.com/oio7DQP2

These markers are different from our food marker

'YES'. The markers for BALL and TUG are also release commands—terminal marker (your dog will need to break position to receive the reward).

You will use this way of reinforcing your dog's behaviour once they have a good understanding of the command we ask.

This will be an interactive way of harnessing your dog's focus and showing them that you can play the game they want if they follow your commands.

Indirectly, while practising this, you will see that you are teaching your dog passive and controlled behaviour to access an active and stimulating reward. I will discuss this form of impulse control later in this book.

For markers to work, you must be clear and concise with your dog. As soon as the marker has been given, you reward the behaviour displayed while the word is said.

Remember, you only have 1.6 seconds for your dog to understand the connection of consequence to behaviour.

Your marker allows you to verbally 'mark' the behaviour and follow through with a reward outside of that 1.6 seconds (as long as you give the marker within 1.6 seconds of the behaviour).

Be mindful of your situation when choosing the appropriate marker your dog can receive.

If you reward your dog for a good down stay at the café, it is best to 'YES' + reward with food rather than 'TUG' and play a game around everyone when trying to have brunch.

When to transition from food to play as reward

https://me-qr.com/CXDDRWw2

Using a clicker

A clicker is a small device that produces a 'click' sound when pressed. This mechanical marker is superior to using your voice as it makes a 100% consistent sound that can be accurate when used correctly. It also sounds the same whether you are excited, feeling flat, or have lost your voice. It is said that a specific part of the brain is activated compared to using your voice which can improve its effectiveness and clarity to the dog, making the training more dynamic and powerful while enhancing your communication.

I teach only some of my clients with a clicker because most pet owners need to be more interested, skilled, or patient to stay consistent using a clicker. It requires some skill to manage food, lead and all other items used in daily life. Also, if you misplace your clicker, you are left without a way to mark your dog's behaviour.

I am happy for people to show interest and use a clicker, and it makes me excited as it offers another level of enthusiasm for the training. You can use the clicker as a marker for whatever you desire (for food, tug, or ball). However, it is best used as a reward and release- terminal marker ('SIT' + CLICK = dog breaks position to receive the reward) and not as a durational marker (stay in behaviour waiting for food to come to them).

The best way is to use all these markers for reinforcement (YES, TUG, FETCH & CLICK). Depending on your environment, the variety allows you to be clear with your dog and have options if you have misplaced equipment. Using the correct reward will depend on how you will reinforce behaviour and what intensity you would like to reward your dog.

Direct and indirect reward

A direct reward is when the reward is in front of your dog, and it is clear that the behaviour they are performing (being taught) is directly associated with the reward.

A typical example of a direct reward is when you lure your dog into a position where the food is in your hand, and you guide and direct the dog into a specific position before marking and rewarding the behaviour. Usually, in the early stages of teaching behaviours, using direct rewards is recommended to save confusion and clarify what you are teaching your dog.

An indirect reward is when your dog performs a behaviour on cue (verbal or non-verbal) when the reward not being directly in front of them. A typical example is when you have used direct rewards to teach a particular behaviour via luring and your transition to offering a gesture (no food in your hand) or a verbal command. Once the dog performs the behaviour, you MARK + REWARD and follow through with giving your dog the reward from your treat pouch.

We give dogs indirect rewards in many ways, and it is crucial in the training phase of a behaviour to help with the reliability, clarity, and effectiveness of training. If you stay in a direct reward training mode for too long, the dog will learn to rely on the visual cue alone, which means in the absence of that reward; your dog may not perform the behaviour you ask for.

Escape and avoidance

Escape & Avoidance conditioning are terms used to explain two different types of learning through using pressure in training to assist with creating reliable behaviours.

Escape learning is a process of operant conditioning, where your dog learns to perform a behaviour to terminate an aversive stimulus through negative reinforcement.

An example is when you issue the command 'SIT', and your dog does not sit on command.

Applying upward pressure on the leash and then immediately releasing the leash pressure when your dog lowers their but on the ground is a type of escape learning.

Avoidance learning is an operant and classical conditioning process where your dog learns to avoid stimuli by performing the learnt behaviour. An example is when you issue the 'SIT'command, and your dog immediately lowers their butt on the ground to avoid the consequence of the leash pressure.

Both words, Escape & Avoidance, seem like harsh words. However, when executed and paired with positive reinforcement, your dog will find clarity in the training commands which help create reliable behaviour, assuming technique, timing, and correct application have been executed.

Structure over routine

Establish a routine when implementing a new system, whether raising a puppy, acquiring a new dog, or just wanting to promote order in your current dog's life.

I define routine as the discipline and adherence to a set of obligations in a predictable and reliable cycle of the same time and place—for example, feeding, walking, and training your dog at the same time and going to the same places regularly.

The issue arises when we cannot, for whatever reason, commit to a particular activity in that same time/place, and we, in turn, disrupt the 'pattern'. When we abruptly change a pattern in the routine, our dogs can become very unsettled in anticipation of the activity to begin or when your dog does not receive what was thought to be 'promised'. We usually see undesirable behaviour manifest as barking, whining, and destructive behaviour becoming more intense.

It is best to start implementing any new system or schedule as part of your training program by establishing a routine, e.g., feeding, walking, training and letting the dogs come inside, etc., at the same reliable time. Once you have created the habit for you and your dog of adhering to the new way of living, it is advisable to adopt 'Structure over Routine' to do all the various activities with and for your dog but shifting when and where you do them.

Switching from 'routine' to 'structure' allows you to have the flexibility of when you do things without your dog expecting to be fed, walked, let inside, where they walk, who they see and even when to go toilet (within reason and ability to your dog).

Structure is about following through with your daily tasks and obligations with the discipline you will adhere to, but at no set time or place. This enhances your relationship with your dog because you will not feel pressured to rush home to commit to an activity because of your dog, and your dog won't display undesirable behaviour demanding to get what they want, which means less stress on both sides of the leash.

An example of how I utilise structure over routine with my dogs is that I feed at different times of the day, sometimes 4 pm, sometimes 10 pm, but usually between 7 and 9 pm. I purposefully do not keep a rigid routine, so my dogs are settled in the evening. Even if I won't be home until later in the evening, I do not need to worry about my dogs barking and stressing because they are expecting their food.

We also walk different routes at different times every day but still practice all training and walking rules to keep the structure of our outings. This allows commands and behaviours to be reliable even if we are in a new and different location.

I understand this can be hard for some people to implement as many people's lives are heavily regimented and follow strict routines (work and school commitments). It can be a matter of walking before breakfast some days and other days walking after breakfast; even a tiny shift can fix the matter of a dog barking at 6 am demanding their food and walking.

Neurologically, our bodies (and dogs, too) will anticipate activity to commence by releasing hormones and chemicals, which can affect mood, behaviour and learning. Therefore, people make the excuse, 'Sorry, I'm in a bad mood; I haven't had my morning coffee yet'. This is not only because coffee makes you feel good but also because your body expects the chemical (caffeine), which has not yet arrived, which makes us agitated due to a physiological process.

A Professor of Neuroscience, Andrew Huberman, explained on his podcast that if you eat three times a day at the exact time daily for five days, on day six, your body will release certain hormones to prepare for the consumption of food, which will leave you feeling agitated, lack of focus and moody. This reinforces the need for 'Structure over Routine' practice.

Adopting the mindset of structure over routine shows that our daily lives (and, of course, our dogs, too) are directly and indirectly affected by our behaviour, habits, and routines. Using this ' structure over routine ' principle, we want to leverage drive and motivation in calculated ways to significantly influence our dog's behaviour.

Please do everything you need to do, but you choose when they happen, not your dog's impulses. We do not want our dogs to be slaves to their desires, we want our dogs to learn to earn what they get through us. This is a part of being a good leader for our dogs.

Impulse control

Impulse control is when your dog learns to resist temptation or an intense desire to engage with a specific stimulus and to learn how to follow commands or behave calmly, as taught, around these fascinating things. Impulse control applies to all areas of training your dog, from learning how to act appropriately in the house around guests to walking the streets with other dogs and exciting things around or even holding a 'DOWN-STAY' until released in a busy environment.

There are many ways of achieving impulse control with your dog, and you will notice that most of our training is about achieving the best control in all areas of life with your dog.

Here is a game you can play with your dog based on introducing or strengthening impulse control for your dog:

- Treat pouch attached or ball/tug (use highest value reward).

- Play with your dog and build up their excitement, run around and roughhouse play.

- As your dog is near the peak of their excitement, issue command, 'YES' to begin.

- As your dog sits, 'YES' + REWARD + RELEASE (either

'OK' if you fed with treats or 'DROP' to release/let go of tug or ball).

- Continue to play and repeat this for a few minutes or at the peak of the training session. Finish on a good note.

As you practice this game with your dog, you can, over time, introduce all your commands and hold the stay for extra duration, just like always going to your dog's pace rather than your expectation of where they 'should' be.

This technique will help in many areas of your dog's life by teaching them to be calm and controlled when random exciting stimulus pops up, e.g., the dog comes from around the corner while you're on walks or when you come home, and your dog is super excited to see you and jumps and barks.

Impulse control games and training help with this type of behaviour which will become apparent as you continue to train them consistently. So, even though your dog is in high drive and excited, you can offer a command ('SIT'), and your dog thinks there is a potential for an even better outcome. Your dog also perceives that even though something appeals to them, they have to control themselves in the presence of it, and we have provided that practice for it. Specifically finding ways to arouse and heighten your dog's drive and then being able to switch your dog into a focused mindset is a big part of developing impulse control. With your dog's focus on you while in a busy environment, your dog may be better able and prepared to understand and follow your direction/command.

For us humans, impulse control is usually taught to us by our parents or teachers to help us concentrate and pay attention to a particular task, even when there are more exciting things to do. In my experience, I learned that breathing techniques and consistent practice not only taught me to be calm when I practised breathing but also helped me be calmer when a situation went south. Instead of panic and fear, I try to become apparent, calm, and focused on responding appropriately.

Most sports and martial arts are great examples of developing impulse control. They provide the time and space where the heart rate increases, the body moves, adrenaline pumps, and we think simultaneously to follow strategy and tactics. In activities like this, our focus is necessary as immediate consequences are present, and life skills develop as we practise these activities and learn to make decisions under stress and pressure. Think about that when you are developing impulse control with your dog.

Feeding guide

Food is and should be a valuable resource to your dog as it is necessary for life. It would be best if you fed your dogs appropriately to honour their biology by seeking a nutritional schedule that meets your dog's needs to allow them to thrive.

I will not address what food you should feed your dog as this is not my field of expertise. However, I will offer suggestions on how to use food to enhance your training and your dog's lifestyle and discuss how I have used food for my dogs.

I generally feed my dogs (dogs over one year old) once a day. They have a mixed diet of primarily raw food diet (mix of muscle meats, organs, pureed vegetables and supplements) along with high-quality dry food (kibble) and raw meaty bones- chicken carcass, turkey neck or beef brisket (once a week as their meal for that day). Other things that make up their diet are not necessary for explanation here.

If you choose to feed your dog from the bowl, you should offer the bowl of food and leave it for 10 minutes. If not eaten, take it away and offer food the following day (or the next allocated feeding time if you feed twice daily).

Dogs are predators, and gorge eaters, which means food is eaten when it is available and worked for; they are not grazing animals and should not have access to food all day long. Leaving food out all day, feeding multiple times a day and feeding scraps at the dinner table create fussy dogs, which is undesirable for the training process.

From personal experience, I know what it is like to have a fussy dog. I made one of my previous dogs, Ace, very fussy cooking his meals, and when he did not eat, I would add all the tasty additions such as canned fish, cat food, gravy, you name it, I added it. It got to the point that he would sniff his food and walk away without taking a bite until I added something to it. I couldn't leave the food out because I had two dogs at the time, as Spades (my other dog) would eat it.

With the advice of a dog trainer I spoke to, I adopted the 10-minute rules; if not eaten during that time, remove it and feed it the next feeding time. I did this for several days and offered the food, but my dog would refuse to eat. I threw the food away and offered it the following day.

After a couple of days, Ace ate his food entirely and never missed a meal. After that, hunger was real, but I had to change the ritual around food. I never withheld food from Ace; I offered food to him, I couldn't leave it out, and I refused to add anything extra inside it. I also ensured he was not sick or injured by visiting a vet to ensure that was not contributing to why he refused to eat.

To maximise the value of food to utilise for training your dog, you should consider these two concepts:

- Train your dog on an existential reward system (daily ration of food comes from the training pouch)

- Or, seek the most valuable food your dog likes (cooked meat or dog roll)

An existential reward system means all your dog's food comes from training, which means you allow for a few windows of opportunity throughout the day to be fed via your training. This means your dog doesn't get fed for free from the bowl and is expected to perform in training time for 'treats'. A hungry dog wants food and will put more effort into the training. You should set your dog up for success and start by feeding this way in low-distracting environments and gradually build on environmental stimuli over the days and weeks following. An existential reward system is the best way to start your training journey, especially if your dog is more food motivated.

The alternative is feeding your dog as usual from the bowl and using high-value soft food (easy for your dog to eat and tasty) for your training. This is easy for dogs with a high food drive. To prevent overfeeding, feed less from the bowl and use nutritional dog rolls to make up for what has been removed from daily feeding time.

When I acquired my new dog Chilli, a one-year-old Australian Koolie, I chose to feed on the existential reward system for two main reasons: to maximise the value of training and my relationship with him and to address some minor fear issues with the new environment. Chilli was bred and raised on a rural property where the environmental stimuli were low compared to where I live. As a result, he was fearful of buses, people holding umbrellas and a few other things. Because of this, I chose to feed Chilli all of his food from my pouch for the first two months, and in this time, I exclusively fed him kibble from my pouch, as it was much easier to handle and occasionally fed him raw food in a KONG™ in that period.

I wanted to make sure that I leveraged food as a fundamental 'currency' to Chilli to be able to work on all our training and to focus on making me the most valuable thing in his life, which immensely helped with desensitising him to his new environment. We were very successful in using food in our training. After those initial two months, I started to feed Chilli as I fed my other two dogs, from the bowl to predominantly feeding raw food and continued to use food in training, either a portion of his daily rations in kibble or dog roll from my pouch. I also used the ball/tug for most of Chilli's training.

Food is a powerful tool in a dog trainer's toolbox. Maximise its value in whatever works best for you and your dog. Make sure you are mindful of your dog's relationship with food, and don't spoil your dog, especially if you are on the journey of training.

Consideration: Some bones can pose risks such as bacterial infections (e.g, Salmonella) and physical injuries (tooth fractures or intestinal blockages). Consult with a certified canine nutritionist prior to implementing a raw diet or feeding raw bones, to ensure safety and nutritional adequacy.

Vet checks/ pressure conditioning

We want our dogs to get used to being touched in all areas of their body so that they become conditioned and tolerate it. If we don't do this in the early stages, it can result in a dog being unable to accept handling in sensitive and sore spots.

This conditioning is critical when visiting the vet and having to be handled when addressing painful wounds, infected areas (ear infections, etc.), having temperature checked (thermometer up the butt), nails clipped and vaccinations.

A rub-down session is an excellent habit, especially from puppyhood and as your dog grows into an adult, because it is bonding time. It is an excellent practice to keep up as you may notice injuries, lumps, bumps, fleas and ticks. You must check to be in tune with your dog's health and wellbeing.

Things to do:

- Have a treat pouch equipped with treats.
- Start rubbing your dog along the back and underside of their body, 'YES' + reward.

- Touching their ears and around the eyes gently, 'YES' + reward.

- Touching and rubbing paws and nails, 'YES' + reward.

- Touching tail and lower areas,'YES' + reward.

- Increase pressure on how firm you touch as you go and as your dog gets used to it.

- Make it a POSITIVE experience!

Conditioned relaxation

Besides desensitising our dogs to being touched all over their body, particularly sensitive areas, getting into a good habit of rub-down and massage as it has many benefits:

- Feels good to loosen muscles/ligaments.

- Be in tune with dysfunctions or abnormalities (lumps, bumps, etc.).

- Encourage a calm state of mind by using a word or physical touch on cue.

- Bonding time between you and your dog. Passive time away from the activity of exercise/training.

Start by finding a relaxing and comfortable area (living room or backyard) where you can commit for at least 20 minutes. Use a word or sound ('chill', 'shh-hh') while doing long, soft- medium pressure from shoulder to tail. Do this in a meditative state, calm, to encourage the feel of the activity.

If your dog does not want to participate and wants to play, encourage them to sit or lay down next to you, with no corrections, and stay persistent. Once you achieve a calm state, continue to cover areas of the body, i.e., legs, ribs & neck. We aim to relax our dogs, to obtain a state of deep rest but not sleep. The rub-down may take 20 minutes or more. Find your rhythm and style, as there are many different approaches.

As a simple guide, our main objective is consistency. Call your dogs over, say your dog's name and start the rub-down. It will take a few minutes to influence your dog to enter this state. But with practice, it will become as easy as a command within a significantly short time.

Training benefits include improving impulse control and teaching your dog that you are the source of both passive and calm activity, along with active and intense training (yin & yang). The bonding experience, along with the opportunity for mindfulness, is priceless.

The word 'chill' will also be an indirect command at home and in public to mean, come close and relax with me. Another form of condition relaxation is when your dog is crate trained. Being inside the crate only represents one thing: lay down, chill out and sleep. The context of being in the crate brings on that calm state of mind, this is an excellent example of a conditioned response.

4

Dog Training Definitions

It is best to introduce terminology and definitions before explaining how to teach and train behaviours. I offer descriptions based on the way I use them in my training. They may differ between other trainers and their systems. It is essential for your dog training success that these terms are clarified, so there will be no confusion. Learning the fundamentals is crucial to executing your training plan.

Continuous reinforcement

Continuous reinforcement is when you offer your dog a reward every time your dog performs a behaviour you are teaching. The goal is to create a positive, exciting, and consistent reward. It will increase the likelihood of your dog committing to that behaviour when still making early connections to a command, behaviour or skill.

Continuous reinforcement is usually when your dog is in the 'Teaching' phase. If you stay on a continuous reinforcement schedule, it is likely that your specific commands will become extinct (the dog stops performing the behaviour). This is because your dog thinks it will always get a reward for performing that behaviour. If you miss a reward a few times, it may stop being reliable when higher distractions are around, and your dog will choose to do something else more desirable than the expected treat.

A good example is a vending machine. It is reliable to say that putting money into the machine will give you the selected item, which works for many repetitions over time. However, one day you spend the same amount of money and choose the same thing, and it doesn't deliver. We get mad and start to hit the machine, move it around and shake it. We leave with frustration. The next day you return to the machine hoping it will deliver, and it does not work again. From then on, we are less likely to return to the same machine in the future because we know we won't get what we want. Not receiving the expected reward can decrease the drive to complete the command or behaviour.

Intermittent reinforcement

Intermittent reinforcement, in most cases, comes after continuous reinforcement. You want to reward your dog sometimes when behaviour is performed. Intermittent reinforcement will increase the effort in how the behaviour is performed and make it less likely for the desired behaviour to become extinct, which means the dog will try hard, especially after not being rewarded.

In the Training Phase, when you ask for a behaviour, e.g. 'Come', and you don't reward it but just praise, then your dog won't be too disappointed and will still come the next time you reissue the recall, which you then will reward. This does not mean skipping every second reward because your dog will figure out the pattern. Always switch it up and ensure you're rewarding the best behaviours.

This schedule of reinforcement produces more dopamine, a natural molecule released in the brain responsible for reward-seeking, anticipation, drive and overall motivation. When done correctly, you can build drive and reliability of behaviour by rewarding intermittently.

A great example and comparison to the continuous reinforcement example above is a poker machine which offers an intermittent reinforcement schedule. The randomisation of the payouts received on the poker machine is what keeps people pressing the button and gambling the money, which is why poker machines are highly addictive. The fact that the reward does not come in multiple turns in a row may mean another reward is on its way. Similarly, in dog training, a variable reward schedule can encourage obedience and increase the chances of success in your training.

We want our dogs to be highly engaged and motivated to perform commands and the associated behaviours. Ensure you keep your dog guessing by rewarding on a randomised schedule.

Variable reward

A variable reward is when you 'JACKPOT' your dog when they perform the behaviour very well or the best, and you give them more food than usual. The best type of jackpot is by rewarding multiple times after the behaviour you wish to occur. An example of this is instead of feeding a handful of food (more in your hand than usual), you can mark and reward three times in a row ('YES' + food,

'YES' + food, 'YES' + food). You can reward variably in continuous or intermittent reinforcement schedules for specific commands or behaviours and in all teaching, training and proofing phases.

A poker machine also fits the example of combining INTERMITTENT and VARIABLE reinforcement schedule. Unlike a vending machine where you know when and what you'll get when you put your money in, with a poker machine, you don't know what you will receive. Most of the time, you don't get a good return; other days, you make your money back plus more, and on rare days, you win big! The randomness of the amount, whether it is more or less , stimulates happy hormones (one of which is dopamine) to be released. The uncertainty of the reward is what makes the games more addictive and pleasurable. When your dog knows a potential reward is available, you see more focus, drive and reliability of behaviour.

Dopamine

Dopamine is the molecule responsible for anticipation, drive and motivation. When your dog has a high drive to perform a behaviour, it is because dopamine is released within your dog's brain in anticipation of the reinforcement. Once the reward has been acquired, dopamine levels drop until the signal or stimulus presents itself again.

Dopamine and its function in the brain and body is quite complex; however, the valuable thing to understand is that it is released in pursuit of the reward, not when achieving the reward. A great example of this is your dog's behaviour when training with a ball. For some dogs, the ball is a very high-value reinforcer—a dopamine releaser—creating a higher level of commitment and drive. If trained properly, leveraging this dopamine release can increase the chances of getting the behaviour that you want in training.

Drive

The term drive is used to describe a dog's level of motivation and behaviour when pursuing reinforcement. It is a state of mind (level of arousal) and is usually, but not exclusive to, a manifestation of prey (predatory) drive seen when a dog wants to chase a ball, play tug or pursue real-life prey.

Food drive is the level of commitment your dog displays when motivated by food—the enthusiasm and intensity to acquire the food. Play drive is the level of motivation and anticipation to play, usually with their handler but also when playing with other dogs.

Reward event

Rewarding a dog is not always as simple as offering the reinforcer (food, ball or tug) to your dog, it should celebrate the behaviour you are teaching your dog and enhance the reinforcing nature of the reward. A reward event is a chain of reinforcing actions that motivate your dog to repeat behaviours, along with creating more engagement in you, which develops a stronger drive and, as a result, more robust behaviour.

An example of a reward event can be utilising our movement

and motion when delivering food to your dog, such as if your dog struggles with recall (come when called). You call your dog over, and as your dog runs toward you with great effort and intensity, you can MARK ('YES') and run backwards while giving multiple treats as you're moving back away from your dog, along with a little rough play session with your dog.

Another example can be rewarding a dog with the ball. You can throw the ball multiple times after they perform the behaviour appropriately to be associated with a better ball session rather than being rewarded with one single throw.

Opposition reflex

Opposition reflex is a natural reflex where most healthy dogs will lean or push against any opposing pressure or stimulus applied to the body. It is a natural reflex most mammals have as a natural defence to prevent them from falling over. We typically see opposition reflex when applying pressure to a dog's collar or harness. The harder you pull back on the dog's collar/harness, the more they naturally push into the equipment, as is the leading cause of leash pulling.

Only give commands once

It is best to develop the habit of only giving verbal commands once, as it provides the best clarity and reliability in your training. Your dog will likely ignore your commands if you habitually give the verbal command multiple times.

As you will learn, dogs are visually oriented, and we teach behaviours via luring and hand gestures, as these signals are very clear in the initial steps of learning behaviours. Only once your dog understands the gesture do we add a verbal cue (command) to allow appropriate conditioning, verbal commands come before issuing known gestures.

When in the training phase of a command, you must either have your dog's attention on you by saying their name or when the command has been issued. Your dog should voluntarily perform the behaviour.

If your dog chooses to ignore your command, you must follow through with some form of pressure for your dog to comply. If your dog regularly ignores your command, you may have yet to teach the command to a level your dog understands, or you are in a highly distracted environment, causing your dog not to comply. If this is the case, repeating commands will only weaken the verbal cue. You may need to go back a step to refine your training to allow your dog to understand what is expected. Repeating commands can become a bad habit, and knowing this from the beginning of your training can save you time and reduce frustration.

Non-verbal and verbal commands

You will notice as you begin training your dog that your dog is a very observant creature, watching our most subtle cues and actions. Their keen observation of us is how we make associations (commands and habits) a big part of our training.

The luring technique will be a means of guiding/shaping your dog into certain positions to allow us to create behaviours and put them on command. We match a gesture or movement with a word to create these commands.

Remember that your dog usually picks up your non-verbal command (hand movement or body posturing) before understanding the verbal command. As we move through the different stages of each command and behaviour, it will be best to make a clear verbal command and slowly move away from our non-verbal command (hand gesture).

When we teach the DOWN command, we lure the dog into position before we use any verbal command. As your dog starts to connect their behaviour and the lure, we will introduce the verbal command. Often, people get stuck and can only get their dog to lie down if they use the gesture (pointing to the ground) rather than the verbal command on its own. There are ways of showing your dog, both verbal and non-verbal, that you will learn in this chapter.

Remember, body language is a big part of communication with your dog, so be sure you know what your gestures and commands mean to your dog. Be clear and take your time with any step shown below, as you may miss a foundational part of your training.

Luring technique

The luring technique is another foundational element to teaching commands. Luring means your dog's nose follows your hand with a treat in it to teach them new things. Practice these actions:

- Have a piece of food in each hand, close your fist, ensuring your dog knows there is food there but cannot take it out of your hand.

- Lure your dog to one side. If they follow your hand with their nose, say 'YES' and reward.

- Do this multiple times. Your right hand moves to the right-hand side, and your left hand moves to the left-hand side.

We do this so that it will become how you will teach your dog the commands that follow. Luring can be a fun game to get your dog engaged with you, increase focus, and generally foster a good attitude in training.

Luring technique

https://me-qr.com/pnz6Ztwy

Luring vs. gesture

There is an essential distinction between luring and giving a gesture:

- Luring- When food is in your hand, the dog follows your hand with their nose. Through luring, we will manipulate our dog's body in certain positions we will eventually call commands.

- Gesture- When a hand/ body posture is presented and used as a cue to a behaviour that your dog has already learnt. A hand gesture with food in it is luring, not a gesture. In this context, it is essential not to get this mixed up as there is a big difference between both, and it is important to understand this first to get the best results.

Critical distance

When discussing the topics of counter-conditioning, desensitisation and reactivity, the term critical distance will appear. It is a crucial component to understand if you wish to gain success with a dog that has issues around specific triggers or stimuli that evoke undesirable behaviour in your dog.

The critical distance is the closest distance a trigger can be to your dog without causing reactive behaviour. For example, another dog can be 5 metres away from your dog, and your dog acknowledges the dog is there without displaying any reactivity. If the dog gets closer, within 4 metres, and your dog begins to bark, lunge or growl, we can say from this situation the critical distance is 5 metres for this dog to other dogs.

The crucial component in understanding your dog's critical distance to any known trigger is that your job is to reduce that critical distance as much as possible, taking all considerations into account, such as your specific goals, what's appropriate, and your dog's capability. A trigger 10 m away is not the same as it is 1 m away. Know what you wish to desensitise your dog to, understand all the variables that come to play, and set your dog up for success.

Leash pressure

Leash pressure is a beneficial technique to practise with your dog as we need to associate pressure on the lead with a positive outcome and a guide to your dog. Leash pressure is a form of physical communication with your dog and is integral to effective leash handling. Ideally, you want to condition and train your dog to know how to turn off pressure applied to their collar to align with what you want your dog to do in that situation. Leash pressure will occur anytime the leash is attached to your dog. With this in mind, you want to utilise this technique to complement your obedience and loose leash walking.

Pressure motivates and releases educates. Leash pressure is the use of negative reinforcement, which means once the pressure of the leash and collar turns on, it encourages the dog to do a particular behaviour to turn off that pressure. So, learning occurs once the pressure is released, not when it is turned on.

For example, when I tell my dog to sit, and he stands up before I release him out of position, I apply firm but not hard pressure up on the leash and hold the tension (usually 2/10 intensity) as soon as his butt touches the ground I release the pressure (escape). This allows my dog to learn how to turn off the pressure, and with consistency, he knows to stay in the SIT to avoid the pressure turning on and potentially get rewarded.

Most dogs have been taught to walk while on the lead and associate pressure on their collar/harness with forward movement (opposition reflex). As they pull toward their desired location, the pressure on the leash is tight, hence the more they lean into the collar, the more pressure is applied, and usually, the pressure of the leash turns off when they get to the other dog, jump on a person or get to a pleasant smell. This is how owners indirectly train their dogs to pull on the leash.

Opposition reflex is when a dog feels pulled off balance, they tend to lean into the collar to remain in balance. This resistance becomes a cue to push away any direction on the lead when we pull on it. You want to teach your dog to move in the direction of the pressure we apply on their collar for effective control, training, and manners on the leash.

Start this technique at home in a familiar environment, free of distractions. Follow these steps:

1. Have your dog ready with their collar attached to the lead and a treat pouch full of food.

2. As your dog is facing you, apply gentle pressure on the lead to the left-hand side.

3. As your dog moves in the same direction as the pressure, 'YES'+ REWARD

4. Do the same to the right-hand side and reward as your dog follows the pressure of the lead.

5. If your dog is resisting the pressure and is pulling away, you may have started with too much pressure.

6. If you are putting the smallest amount of pressure and the dog is resisting, don't let go and start again; keep the small amount of pressure on until they move towards the direction. If your dog is confused, help out by keeping the pressure on and combining luring with an excited voice to help encourage them. Then once your dog moves even one step, release pressure and simultaneously give a 'YES' + REWARD.

You will see why this is effective when you're out and about, like when you're in a tight spot, moving your dog in and out of the car or maneuvering around high-value distractions. We want our dogs to know precisely what we desire of them. It is unrealistic to food lure your dog in every situation, but if your dog is on the lead, you can guide them with minor leash pressure without resistance and with confidence and control.

For example, when sitting at the coffee shop and you wish to move your dog out of someone's way and position your dog to the left of the table, you can use leash pressure to direct your dog into the desired spot. This can be easy and clear to your dog and is an excellent practical form of communication.

The next step

- Once your dog knows to follow the pressure of the lead, you can use this to move your dog around you to any side of you, followed by 'YES' + REWARD.

- Also, leash pressure up two steps of stairs, 'YES'+ REWARD.

- Into the car, 'YES' + REWARD.

This is not intended for you to drag your dog where you want them to go, this is designed to guide your dog. Clear communication comes from consistency and understanding. When using any form of pressure, you must be careful to use the correct amount and remain calm and firm. Use short sessions, and always finish on a good note.

A common problem people have with this technique is they apply a low level of pressure, 1/10 intensity, and the dog leans against it. Then the person tends to use more pressure 3/10, which makes the dog resist more; they further add more intensity, 5/10 by then, and it gets to the point the dog is experiencing far too much leash pressure and jumps to fight the leash. As soon as a dog starts bucking and fighting, they release the pressure so that they do not choke their dog. The dog learns to turn off the pressure by jumping and biting the leash, which is unsuitable for our technique. In this example, the intensity of the pressure went too high in a concise amount of time, causing stress, teaching the dog the wrong behaviour, which resulted in the pressure being released.

To remedy this, it is best to do it correctly. Keep the 2/10 pressure on. If your dog resists, increase only the duration of pressure, not the intensity. If you wait two seconds and see it through, your dog will understand the only way to turn off the pressure is by moving in its direction. Increasing the intensity of the pressure can be done at one increment at a time. An example is, if 2/10 with some duration is not adequate, 3/10 may encourage your dog to sit. Your dog will be confused if you jump to higher intensity too quickly.

If your dog struggles to understand what the leash pressure means, you can help by luring them in that direction. In contrast, if you maintain pressure and your dog turns off the pressure by taking a few steps in that direction, your next step would be to mark and reward.

Leash pressure technique

https://me-qr.com/DkeRfTtv

Name game

The name game is a technique in which we want to increase the dog's drive, focus and engagement towards you as the handler. The outcome of this technique is to:

1. 'Charge' your dog's name so they understand we are calling to get their proper attention on us.

2. Train your dog to follow the direction of leash pressure when they feel it on their collar instead of dogs pulling against the collar when they feel the pressure (opposition reflex).

3. Increase the dog's drive in a controlled way which will help with issuing commands. Calling your dog's name before giving a command should make the dog

perform the command with more power, precision, speed, and intention. We want the dog's name to announce that something good/fun may follow. This increases the dopamine in the dog, enhancing our training and the dog's focus on us.

Many owners tend to use their dog's name for too many things, such as recall, attention, punishment, praise, getting off the couch, etc. When in times of urgency and calling your dog's name for their attention, your dog's name does not properly register as something you intend it to be at that moment.

You want your dog to hear their name and expect you to give directions immediately after. For example, Daisy runs across the road as we call out 'Daisy'. Daisy looks at us, and immediately, we say 'DOWN'. We walk to them and securely clip the leash.

Rather than calling your dog's name, they immediately run back to you; this can be dangerous if they were to run onto the road.

Alternatively, if you say your dog's name, and they continue to run and ignore you, there's a problem that needs to be corrected.

If you have your dog's focus, you will likely be successful with any commands in any situation.

It would be beneficial if the dog understands the leash pressure technique before working on the name game'. While your dog is on their lead/collar and is focused on a low distracting stimulus ahead of you, whether it is a piece of food on the ground or a person your dog likes:

1. Apply pressure (2 out of 10 intensity) BEFORE saying your dog's name.

2. While keeping pressure on (not increasing intensity), take a few steps back.

3. The second your dog looks back at you, relieve the leash pressure and simultaneously mark 'YES'. Let your dog COME TO YOU to receive a reward, DO NOT move towards your dog to give a reward.

4. To make the game more intense and exciting, continue to run back after marking 'YES' so your dog chases you to receive their reward. Turn the food drive into a play drive, this makes the game more interactive than just feeding your dog for looking at you. This 'GAME' increases the dog's drive and engagement. Use this for when dogs are focused on everything else around them and reactive to other stimuli to bring more power to your commands.

Common mistakes owners make

- **Rewarding the dog for coming to them.** The 'Name Game' is NOT recall training. You reward the dog for looking at you. Only when your dog looks at you is when you mark so that your dog comes to you to receive the reward.

- **When to put leash pressure on and when to remove it.** It seems like a small detail, but it is everything in this technique. Pressure on you is a tactile way of communicating to the dog, to show them to move in the direction of pressure; they know when they have done it correctly when the pressure goes away.

- The leash pressure in the name game is not a correction, this is a guiding force. It also works so that when the dog is in a heightened state of mind, the dog feels the pressure more clearly than hearing your words. If appropriately conditioned, we can use the leash as an effective way of communication.

- **The Name Game only gets the dog to look at you.** You are using this to improve your dog's overall focus and engagement on you. Your goal is to put pressure on and say your dog's name; the moment your dog looks at you, the pressure turns off, followed by giving a command (DOWN). The name game helps get focus, so we don't have to give commands more than once, and it improves the dog's attentiveness on you when dealing with leash reactivity.

Name game technique

https://me-qr.com/7o3xvjHi

Spatial pressure

Spatial pressure in training focuses on the space between you and your dog. It's the technique of using your body to apply negative reinforcement to make your dog comply with commands or direction. It's the act of applying social pressure to create space or can encourage a submissive state of mind in a dog if the dog is sensitive to spatial pressure.

The application of spatial pressure is used as an alternative to leash pressure or any other kind of tool when communicating with your dog.

It is natural for your dog to acknowledge what you are trying to communicate, so finding the best form of communication that fits your dog is critical to training success.

Some breeds are more sensitive to spatial pressure than others; for example, Border Collies and similar types of working breeds are much more attuned and sensitive to you walking into their space compared to Terriers, such as Bull Breeds and Jack Russels that are generally pushier by nature. Be mindful of your dog and how they perceive how you are applying spatial pressure, and use it according to your communication.

Utilising spatial pressure, has different applications; controlling the space, following through with a command or settling your dog and gaining full attention and appeasement from your dog.

For example, when trying to keep your dog from running

through a doorway, instead of pulling your dog back by the collar, screaming random commands or trying to slide through the door gap, you can apply spatial pressure. By standing between your dog and the door, face your dog and use your body to apply annoying pressure until your dog backs up (typically sits).

If your dog ignores your SIT command and you take a slow, steady step towards the dog and it sits, , take a step back to relieve the pressure you created. Another example is if your dog is barking at a passing dog from inside the house, next to your glass door, issue a verbal cue to stop and apply spatial pressure until your dog sits, lays down or shows significant calm behaviour before walking away to relieve the spatial pressure.

3 D's: distance, duration, distraction

The 3 D's are to be considered mainly for durational commands (sit stays, down stays, bed commands). This is because the three main things that determine whether your dog is going to break position are:

- if they have been left in the same position for too long and are not conditioned to remain there for that amount of time,

- how far you have moved from your dog or if you have moved out of sight of your dog, and

- how much distraction is happening around your dog.

For example, you have been working a down stay for the

last month, and your dog can hold a down position until being verbally released for 1 minute, and you can move 5 metres from your dog while on a long lead in your front yard successfully. Your dog may not be ready to hold position without breaking if you walk out of the front gate to your car and back for 20 seconds, or your dog may not be able to hold position while another dog walks past your front yard.

The best thing to do in a durational command is to grow all 3 D's proportionately; this will help with the overall strength of your commands, especially if you need your dog to follow your instructions when you are out and about.

You will need to drill all 3 D's in many forms & combinations to help generalise this to your dog. For example, when practising down stays in a moderately busy environment, it's best to mix up how long your dog stays down and how far you move away a little differently each time. You don't want your dog to assume when you will release them out of the DOWN.

I have taught my dogs Spades and Chilli to hold a down stay in front of a client's house in the shade for up to 1 hour while I am inside the house, out of sight, in a place he has never been. I achieved this over the years through calculated training and consistently growing all 3 D's with the down command.

I was able to achieve this quicker than most, not because my dog is better than anyone else's dog but because I need this behaviour and reliability from him as a trainer. Leaving a dog in a hot car is unacceptable; bringing him into the client's house is not an option, so what I do is suitable for all of us, and Spades is happy and content with it.

I get far more opportunity to practise my training daily as my dogs spend most full days with me, compared to most dog owners; this is important to note as you want to avoid injecting too much of a high expectation too early in training.

Before working and training any command, try to set a goal of what you will like your dog to do and why. This is important because you need to know the direction of your training sessions to avoid getting bored, ultimately setting you and your dog up for failure. Train your dog for practicality and purpose first, then add the extra tricks for fun. You need practical and reliable obedience commands to guarantee safety for your dog, not to mention the joy of having a dog that will listen to you.

Duration:

- Duration is the first of the D's to be practised. You want your dog to stay in a position for up to 5-10 seconds before taking a step away.

- Duration and distance are somewhat intertwined; naturally, the farther you walk from your dog, the longer your dog needs to remain in position. Start building on your duration while your dog is in command in the early phases of your training. It is easy for you to be closer to your dog, and you can reward them continuously for maintaining position, rather than working distance in the beginning.

- Remember what has been advised above. Try to grow

all 3 D's together as they complement each other. From early on, as you can achieve a sit for 5 seconds, start moving the feet to get ready for 5 seconds and a step.

- Our goal when training dogs doesn't necessarily mean staying in a down stay while I walk precisely ten steps in a particular direction; our goal is that 'DOWN' means 'DOWN' until released, regardless of where you walk and for how long. Keep this in mind when you are working duration that the time you want your dog to hold position should not always be the same. Switch it up. For example, over a week of the down stay, switch up the down stay command from 20 seconds, 3 seconds, 45 seconds, 10 seconds, etc. Keep your dog guessing and waiting for the release command, not the amount of time.

Distance:

- When training your dog with a durational command, implement reasonable distance between you and your dog. A good goal is 10 m, as it is the length of the long leads I use. Also, it is a reasonable distance. More than that is not practical in our urban environment.

- You also want your dog to maintain the position if they cannot see you; start by walking around them, going behind a tree, a wall or objects in the environment.

- Remember to gradually increase distance by

rewarding smaller increments at a time and always finishing on a good note. If you go too far from your dog too quickly, your dog will break position and likely run to you. The farther you are, the harder it is to correct them and put them back in place. If you jump from 2 m to 10 m overnight, you are likely to fail & set your dog up for failure; we want our dog to feel in control and have a sense of winning.

Distraction

We must teach durational commands while your dog is motivated and distracted by other things in the environment. Training around distractions is a part of impulse control which is an important part of training your dog. The truth is, once your dog is out of the house, exciting things are everywhere; you want your dog to focus on you and maintain control.

Once your dog is ready to train around distractions as part of your training routine, you should become aware of your dog's distractions, the distance they need to be to become a problem, and good management always on the lead, collar or in a secure area). If you let your dog get success by breaking the 'BED' command to jump on your visitors early in training, you are likely to struggle in future situations; always be prepared!

The point here is that your dog should ideally not be distracted as you should be the most important and fun thing in the world, but in the real world for everyday dog owners, we know our dogs love chasing birds, cats, balls, sounds, etc.

Set your dog for success. While in the duration command, start with adequate distance between your dog and distractions.If the dog across the road creates too much distraction for your dog, then make more space or try when the dog is farther away.Make a note for next time and plan your training to get closer to these sorts of stimuli. Take your time—baby steps to success rather than giant leaps of failure.

Always start your training in a familiar low-distraction environment, and gradually, as your dog moves through each phase, increase the level of activity and stimulus around you and your dog. Know when to ask for a command and when you or your dog are not ready.

5

Obedience Training

The following content is a general review of basic obedience typically covered in a training session. It is used to improve your perspective and introduce the overall system. Techniques may vary depending on each dog/handler combination. Each command will be in its phase. Refer to this often to clarify where you are in your training.

The four most essential commands are SIT, DOWN, RECALL and BED. Focus your training efforts on these four commands prior to addressing the rest of the list of behaviours to teach your dog.

*Before attempting any of the following content of teaching behaviours, make sure you read the whole step-by-step process.

**Rewarding always means giving the marker first.

Three phases of training: Teaching, training and proofing

Each command or behaviour being taught will be in either one of the following phases. The teaching (also referred to as the learning) phase is when the behaviour is taught from the beginning. The training phase is when the dog knows the behaviour and they are learning that we require them to perform a command in new environments. This is the time when the 3 Ds are being implemented and gradually increasing, creating reliable responses to the command. The proofing phase is when the dog totally understands the behaviour and will perform the behaviour reliably in all new environments and can also have a functional application.

Teaching/learning phase:

- Dog is learning the behaviour right from the beginning.

- This is the beginning process of teaching your dog the behaviour planned. We generally use only hand signals and luring in this phase. Once your dog starts showing that they understand what you are teaching via lure and body language alone, then incorporating the word/command is necessary to enter the next phase.

- Ensuring you are in a familiar environment with no distractions so your dog remains focused on you and the training.

- Sessions should be very short when teaching new skills. More frequent and shorter sessions are much more beneficial than less frequent long sessions.

- Continual reinforcement for performing the desired behaviour, which means reward every time your dog performs the behaviour or shows effort towards the behaviour.

- Start introducing verbal commands once your dog understands the behaviour you are teaching them via luring. The word must come before you lure them into position—this is classical conditioning. The new signal must come before the old (already known) signal. For example, if your dog lays down ten times in a row when you lure it down, you can start saying 'DOWN' before you begin to lure into DOWN. If you say the word 'DOWN' after luring begins, your dog will take more notice of the gesture than the word (called overshadowing). We want the verbal command to announce we are about to lure in a certain way so that we can eventually use the verbal command only without hand gestures.

- NO PUNISHMENT or force in the teaching phase, you cannot correct/punish your dog for something they do not know.

- Remember that dogs pay more attention and pick up on gestures before and more reliably than verbal commands. A well-known dog training saying is, 'Don't name it until you love it', which means having a definite meaning of hand gesture/body language cue before issuing verbal commands, and before moving on to the training phase.

Training phase:

- Dog has learnt the behaviour. Now we want clarity and reliability.

- You must have an established verbal command to be in the training phase for the specific behaviour.

- Start introducing some distractions and changing the environment in which you practise the taught behaviour you are working on. For example, if you are training the 'DOWN' command, once your dog reliably performs the behaviour in the backyard, you can move on to the driveway, in the front yard and eventually onto the street, etc. Gradually throughout training you increase the level of external distractions and motivations to your dog in your surroundings.

- Start rewarding intermittently (not giving a treat every time the dog performs behaviour and only rewarding randomly). This will strengthen the behaviour. If you reward every time all the time and one day stop rewarding your dog, then most likely, they will stop performing that specific behaviour reliably and on command. Rewarding intermittently will increase the dog's motivation to perform the behaviour and frequency of behaviour when asked by rewarding your dog's effort and by rewarding the best results your dog offers. Introducing 'maybe' into the equation increases the dog's enthusiasm and makes them try harder for their reward. Increasing motivation and drive is the idea that will strengthen your training commands.

- Chaining behaviours together 'SIT', 'COME', 'DOWN', and YES + REWARD. Rewarding after asking for a combination of commands is also intermittent reinforcement, and it is encouraged to continue to mix it up in training. You do not want your dog to expect a reward will come after every single command but will come 'randomly' (as long as you know which phase each command is in).

- Now that your dog understands the behaviour, if they are ignoring your command and are distracted, it can come from two things. Either you are too close to high distractions, and your dog stops focusing on the training at hand, or you may have gone too far too quick in introducing new distractions. If this occurs, you will need to move your dog to a space where they feel comfortable/less distracted. Alternatively, your dog may ignore you and not value what you are saying, as they may be focused on other things occurring around such as a dog, prey animal or people. Only reward if your dog performed the behaviour you issued.

- Only give commands to your dog ONCE! If you are in an environment/situation where your dog is overwhelmed by things around him, get him focused before asking something of him.

- Introducing leash pressure or a correction may be a practical option. If you are teaching SIT-STAY with your dog, and you take a step forward, and your dog breaks position, you can apply some pressure on the collar upwards until your dog returns to the SIT. Or, in the same scenario, after stepping forward and your dog stands out of the seat, a verbal 'UH-UH' + a quick pop on the lead and your dog then immediately sits can also be the consequence introduced in this phase of their training. Seeking good help by a reputable competent balanced trainer, with pressure and correction may be necessary to ensure you're doing it with the correct intensity, frequency, and timing.

Proofing phase:

- Dog understands the behaviour and must perform the behaviour in all environments and be able to do this off lead.

- We are now in the final and ongoing stage of training. Your dog should be reliably performing the command/behaviour we have trained them to do with verbal commands only.

- Adding distractions of other dogs, loud sounds, bike riders, cars, boats, people and other stimuli/distractions that you will most likely encounter with your dog.

- Some dogs are desensitised to cows and horses because they see them every day, whereas a city dog may instinctively chase at first sight of stock.

- We generally only reward the best behaviours in this phase and must apply a form of correction if we have non-compliance.

- If your dog ONLY does something for a treat, then this is not practical and means you are not in the proofing phase. If your dog encounters something more exciting and wants to run towards it, we want them to understand there is a consequence for not following commands. This will mean you go back to the training phase.

- By this stage, you will be able to command your dog to do what you have taught on a long lead, in a park full of plenty of distractions, with only a verbal command or off lead in the appropriate location.

- The proofing phase is the desired phase we want all the commands we teach to be. Your dog will only reach this level with practise, patience and persistence—you must be consistent! If you wish to get your dog to this level, practise daily and follow the rules.

- Remember, every dog is different, so do not compare your dog to other dogs you have had or seen, only compare your dog to their past performance and the level they were at yesterday. This is the key to excellence.

- Even if your dog has proofed commands, if you've lost consistency or they develop new motivations from external stimuli, you may need to go back to the training phase.This is alright;it is a part of management and consistency.

- There is no 'fully trained dog.' You will still need to reinforce behaviours intermittently. Otherwise, the dog will either stop performing (behaviour goes extinct) or if you rely on too much punishment, you will create stress and confusion. Make sure you have the dog following command in the hope that a reinforcer MAY follow.

- Your dog should feel that if they follow a command, a reward may be issued (an effect of intermittent reinforcement). Your reward may not always be food, ball or praise, it may be access to the park, person or dog (whatever your dog finds reinforcing in that moment).

- Reinforcement only sometimes comes as a reward (food, ball, tug, pat). It comes in the form of what the dog wants in that particular moment (release to run free in the park, to play with other dogs, be let inside, or even get a good pat).

- Every situation is different, but this is only a generalised guide to explain these phases of learning.

Commands are as follows:

- **SIT**
- **DOWN**
- **RECALL**
- **BED**
- **LOOK**
- **TOUCH**

- **LEAVE IT**
- **DROP**
- **MIDDLE**
- **HEEL**

Teaching 'SIT' command:

- With the treat in your hand, make sure your dog knows you have the food (smell it with their nose).

- From a standing position, lure the treat from their nose over their head and toward their bottom.

- This will naturally make their body go into a sitting position.

- Once your dog's butt touches the ground, say 'YES' and give the treat.

- At first, you do not say 'SIT', you want your dog to understand what behaviour you want using the luring technique.

- Practise this process a few times and finish on a good note.

- Once you feel that your dog understands the hand gesture (luring) and can perform the command ten times out of ten, IN A ROW, you can start introducing the verbal command 'SIT' to the physical action. Say the word 'SIT' one second before luring so that the new verbal command predicts the lure, which makes the behaviour occur.

- Reward multiple times while your dog is sitting in position. Between each reward, stand back straight before giving the marker and feeding.

- If your dog is now waiting in a sit position between rewards, say 'OK' and feed away from your dog so that they release out of position.

- Now it is time to take a single step away from your dog, between rewards and before you release ('OK'). If your dog breaks before the release, do not feed. Issue the command 'SIT' again and repeat with a step away before rewarding and releasing.

- Introduce stepping in different directions so that your dog knows to stay in the SIT regardless of which direction you step towards.

- Introducing leash pressure will help you maintain reliability and compliance with the command in the training phase. Show your dog that light pressure on your dog's collar in an upward motion (up to the sky) is also a cue to SIT.

- To introduce the pressure properly, start by having your dog's collar or slip lead on, apply very subtle 1/10 pressure on the collar upwards 90 degrees half a second before giving the verbal command 'SIT' and help with your lure. The second your dog SITS, immediately release the leash pressure and mark simultaneously. Ensure your dog understands that the pressure will go away as soon as they sit.

Training 'SIT':

- Have your treat pouch full of tasty food.

- Have a collar and leash on your dog.

- Make sure your dog is next to you on the left-hand side, facing the same direction you are.

- With NO food in your hand, say 'SIT', then make the gesture (hand above the dog's head).

- As soon as your dog sits, say 'YES' before reaching your pouch and feeding. Ensure you are not telegraphing gestures before giving verbal commands (word before hand gesture).

- Continue to step away after giving verbal commands. Once your dog understands to stay sitting while you step away until you give a release command, you can introduce a second step.

- If your dog breaks position, apply and hold continuous leash pressure, not too intense, just uncomfortable (usually 2/10 intensity) in an upwards direction on the collar until your dog places their butt back on the ground.

- If your dog struggles with this, reward immediately after the butt touches the ground. Typically, no reward comes after correction.

- Release ('OK') if your dog stays in the sit position.

- Start adding more steps until you can walk a circle around your dog.

- Move from a familiar environment (inside your house/backyard) to where there are more distractions (move to the front yard, footpath, park, etc.).

- In the training phase, you can now use a ball or tug as a reward, as long as your dog is clear about what 'SIT' means and will stay until released.

- Remember to use a specific marker for the particular reward ('FETCH' = BALL), the marker for ball or tug is a release out of the behaviour. E.g., tell the dog to 'SIT', take a step away, 'FETCH', and throw the ball. When using the ball to reward, there is no need to say 'YES' or 'OK'.

- Reward intermittently (randomly) for the good SITS. Ensure you don't feed too predictably and too often as you both improve.

- Do not ask too many commands or too often without feeding, as phasing out food too early is a common mistake.

- Always reward good effort from your dog and any incremental improvement towards your specific goals and overall attitude from previous training sessions.

Releasing a dog from a SIT

https://me-qr.com/RTCZnfGo

Introducing leash pressure for breaking SIT

https://me-qr.com/RTCZnfGo

Proofing 'SIT'

When using the SIT command as a ritual and habit, you should tell your dog to sit before walking through doorways, crossing the road, before mealtime, waiting around while on the leash, etc.

If your dog does not follow your commands, correct him. Use the verbal punishment marker 'UH-UH' before following through with leash correction. Over time, you will only need to give a verbal marker, and your dog will understand and comply in a proofed phase of SIT.

The SIT is the most straightforward behaviour to proof as it is usually practised and occurs daily as a functional command. Most people proof the SIT without noticing or trying to make it happen, depending on how much it gets used and its function.

Teaching 'DOWN'

Teaching the DOWN command is one of the top 3 commands your dog must understand, especially if you wish to experience more activities and time out of the house. The DOWN allows you to communicate with your dog to lay down on command and to remain in position until you release your dog out of position.

The DOWN is a durational command, and your dog must perform and remain in position with the 3D's (Duration, Distance and Distraction) in action. If you want your dog to stay in one spot for longer than 5 minutes, then the DOWN is much preferred over SIT, as dogs do not want to hold a squat position for a prolonged period, whereas your dog can lay down for hours when resting. Off-leash privileges are to be given to your dog if they can hold a DOWN until you verbally release and COME when called (recall) from high-level distractions.

The DOWN is lifesaving if your dog was to run across the road. You do not, in this circumstance, recall your dog as it doubles their chances of being hit by a car. The DOWN will ensure that you can go to your dog and leash them or take them to a safer place. The DOWN is also functional when you are enjoying lunch at the café, waiting for the kids to finish the sports game and many other practical uses that make your life with your dog more enjoyable and less stressful.

Nose-to-toes technique

Start with a handful of multiple treats, and with your dog standing, lure from the nose and down the chest between your dog's paws. You may not get this the first time, but ensure you continue to reward effort towards your first step, getting your dog's elbows to touch the ground. This is why having multiple pieces of food in your hand is essential to maintain the dog's focus on your hands despite already being rewarded. Make sure to continue to reward your dog's effort rather than expecting the end result to occur immediately.

When your dog lowers its elbows to the ground even though his butt is still in the air, make sure to reward, as the requirements to the DOWN command consist of both elbows and butt firmly on the ground. The tip to this is to keep your luring hand still and between your dog's front paws on the ground. If you move your hand in reaction to your dog, they will certainly stand up to figure out a way to receive the food. Keeping the luring hand firm and still will encourage your dog to maintain elbows on the ground.

If you're still rewarding the effort, your dog will either stand up or lower their butt to the ground. When they fall into the absolute position (butt and elbows on the ground), jackpot your dog with more food than usual in multiple food rewards. If they stand up, repeat this process, and never reward your dog for standing up. Only reward attempts closer to the result.

The nose-to-toe method is trickier to teach initially, but it has two significant benefits compared to the alternative (the L Method below):

1. It is clearer to the dog that 'DOWN' is elbows + butt on the ground right from the beginning. Teaching the DOWN command from the SIT position is easier, but in time can cause some confusion as the 'SIT' likely becomes a cue to DOWN (some dogs will lay down when they hear the 'SIT' command), and your dog may only know to lay down from a sitting position. Our final goal is to issue the Down command while your dog is walking and can lay down on cue immediately.

2. The nose-to-toe technique encourages the dog to lay in a 'sphinx' position rather than the dog lying down on its hip.

L method

If you struggle to get your dog to lay down with the nose-to-toe technique, try the L method, which starts from a SIT (do not say 'SIT', lure your dog into a sit position). Lure food from the nose down the chest to your dog's front paws and reward. If your dog stands up here, start from the beginning.

Once your dog is still in the SIT position and has lowered the body to get the food, continue to lure away from your dog's paws slightly, allowing them to move paws forward and elbows touch the ground. Again, reward effort (butt still on the ground while the dog is following the lure to encourage your dog to keep trying); when elbows touch the ground, jackpot.

Once your dog lays down 10 out of 10 times reliably from luring (either with nose to toes or L method), you can start to introduce the verbal command before luring your dog ('DOWN'). Remember, 'don't name it until you love it' to be clear that the word DOWN predicts the lure/gesture.

Ensure the verbal command is said one second before luring into position. We want the verbal command to announce the lure. Over time, the verbal command becomes a reliable cue, and the gesture of pointing to the ground will become obsolete.

The next step is having multiple pieces of food in your luring hand, and while kneeling, give the command 'DOWN' and, a second later, lure into the down position. After rewarding your dog in the DOWN, quickly and swiftly move your lure hand to your lower back and IMMEDIATELY offer a MARK + REWARD.

Repeat this process multiple times. This is a crucial step because dogs see life in pictures, and our hand on the ground while kneeling seems to be the known 'signal' to the dog.

We want to incrementally reward while you are in different postures to teach your dog that DOWN means the dog's butt and elbows are touching the ground, and it's not our hand position that is the reliable signal.

It is essential to mark ('YES') when your hand is behind your back before giving the food to your dog. We want to teach your dog that your hand moving away is why the reward occurred, which will allow us to increase the duration of our hand away from your dog to allow us to move to the next step.

A common mistake and issue owners have is that they successfully get in the DOWN position with their lure; however, as soon as their hand moves away and their back straightens up, the dog breaks out of the DOWN. To combat this, we must teach a release command from the DOWN so that your dog will learn that staying in position will continue to pay until a release command ('OK') is issued. This is a good habit for both humans and dogs to develop early in training to ensure it is effective as the training process continues.

Before moving to the next step, increase the duration (up to 3 seconds) of your hand behind your back so your dog is waiting for the marker ('YES') to be fed or the release ('OK') to break position. Ensure the release command is said before luring your dog out of position.

While the dog is in the DOWN and your hand is behind your back, slowly straighten your knees to a half-standing position. When you're in this position, MARK + REWARD and if your dog breaks position, repeat and do not feed for breaking position without a release command.

Incrementally, stand more straight over several sessions to be able to reward after issuing 'DOWN', moving the hand, and finally standing up. You should be able to do this over a few days to a week, where your dog is still lying down while you're standing up straight, either waiting for a marker or release command.

The following steps are to incorporate this command on many different surfaces around the house, starting on carpet or wet grass, and over time, with confidence and clarity of the command, introduce floorboards and tiles, as some dogs may find this challenging.

Introducing leash pressure will help you in the training phase of maintaining reliability and compliance with the command.

Show your dog that light pressure on their collar in a downward motion is also a cue to lay down.

To introduce the pressure properly, start by having your dog's collar or slip lead on, apply very subtle 1/10 pressure on the collar downwards to the ground half a second before giving the verbal command 'DOWN' and help with your lure.

The second your dog lays down (elbows and butt on the ground), immediately release the leash pressure and mark simultaneously. Ensure your dog understands that the pressure will go away as soon as they lie down.

You want the pressure to be a new cue to the dog that it means lying down on the ground. If your dog starts to resist, it is because you haven't conditioned leash pressure enough (see Leash Pressure Technique) or you are applying too much pressure.

The downward pressure to the ground should be a guide, not a forceful action. The low-level pressure must stay on until your dog goes into the desired position. Do not release tension when your dog resists, and do not wrestle your dog to go into the down position.

The purpose here is to layer pressure into the process to

be another way of communicating with your dog. If you're struggling with this, go back a step and take your time.

In this learning phase, you want to avoid causing conflict for the command with your dog. If you are successful, you will notice that your dog will lie down as soon as you apply downward pressure on the leash towards the ground.

- With your dog in a sit position, lure by moving your hand with the treat down along their chest. Ensure their nose follows your lure hand and your luring hand is full of multiple pieces of food.

- If they are finding it difficult, then reward increments of the whole behaviour so they understand that following your hand is what makes them get the reward.

- Once their elbows touch the ground, say 'YES' + REWARD.

- Once your dog is in the down position, move your hand away (toward your back) quickly and IMMEDIATELY reward him—teaching your dog that the longer they stay down, the more they get rewarded. Ultimately, you want to be able to give the command and stand straight before offering a reward.

- Do not incorporate the verbal command 'DOWN' until your dog performs the behaviour independently, 10 times out of 10, in a row via luring.

- Techniques may vary as some dogs learn the down

command through other methods.

Teaching DOWN

https://me-qr.com/UGqMNRqK

Training 'DOWN'

Ensure the leash is attached to your dog's collar or slip leash is attached. Keep your dog on the left-hand side and start training inside the house, backyard or low-distraction environment.

We want to get into good habits and keep your dog facing the same direction as you while they remain on your left-hand side.

Our first step in the training phase of the DOWN command is introducing an empty hand gesture and stopping luring the dog into a DOWN position. Start by putting multiple pieces of food in your non-luring hand and keep the other hand you usually lure empty.

While your dog is attentive to you, say your dog's name, give the verbal command 'DOWN' one second after, and offer the gesture (with no food in hand) down to the ground (as if you were using the lure).

As soon as your dog lays down with a gesture, immediately reward your dog with the other hand with food.

The function of this step is to move from a direct reward, a dog following food in hand (lure), to an indirect reward (empty hand gesture).

Moving from direct to indirect reward is crucial because if you do not introduce this now, your dog will only lie down following food (after smelling your hand) and refuse to follow commands as they think they are supposed to follow food.

In the teaching phase, the food makes the behaviour occur; in the training phase, you want to teach your dog that the behaviour makes the food occur.

Once you successfully issue verbal commands and use only a gesture to complete the behaviour, it is time that all food stays in the pouch while training the DOWN. Keeping food in your hand tells your dog that you have food, which can affect this process as they may only perform commands if there is food in your hand. We want to implement real-life circumstances in the training phase to help create reliable and precise commands.

It is important to remember that in the training phase, you must reward INTERMITTENTLY and not every single time your dog lays down on command. Rewarding random DOWNS, rewarding random durations, rewarding varying amounts of steps, and rewarding random distractions that present themselves are critical. Being too predictable with reward will lessen the command's strength and cause it to lose value over time. Keep your dog guessing and in anticipation of potential reward so that over time your frequency of rewarding becomes less for the practicality and reliability of the behaviour.

Now, issue a verbal command; one second later, give a gesture down towards the ground, stand up, and say 'YES', one second later, retrieve food from the pouch and feed your dog. If at any time during this step, your dog breaks before you give food or release out of position before issuing a release command, say 'NO' and apply low-level leash pressure to the ground. Leash pressure is essential if you wish to correct your dog for breaking position early. The consequence for breaking position early is that we make our dog 'correct' by compelling the dog to go back into the DOWN until we release out of position.

Once you can correct your dog for breaking position early, we introduce a step away from our dog. After issuing a command and your dog lays down, take a tiny step forward. If your dog stays in position, immediately MARK + REWARD by stepping back into your starting position (next to your dog). If your dog breaks when you step or hear the marker, say 'NO' and apply leash pressure to correct your dog and put them back in the DOWN position.

If you successfully take a step forward and return to reward, release your dog ('OK') and reward. Remember to always finish on a positive note and do not rush your training. It is better to take a few days and keep spirits high for both you and your dog. If you ask for too much, too soon, your dog won't want to do the behaviour or, worse, check out and not want to train with you due to confusion or conflict which results in your dog stressing out.

Healthy amounts of stress are necessary for growth, too much will hinder growth and your relationship. We want these activities to build your relationship while making it fun and practical, so your dog learns to comply with the new boundaries.

Once you achieve a 10/10 success with taking one step away from your dog in a familiar and low-level environment, you are ready to implement training at the front door, front yard, and driveway and introduce it on the walk (in comfortable and lower-level distraction environments). Set your dog up for success, and only ask a little in these early stages of generalising this command.

As you find that your dog will stay in position while you can step away, introduce a single step in different directions (one step to the right, diagonal right and back). Show your dog that the DOWN means stay regardless of the direction you step to maintain practicality and set up for the next step. Your dog may get confused and break when you step in a new direction; remember, dogs see the world through pictures, and when something changes in what your dog sees, you may get a different response.

If you and your dog are successful with you stepping in new and different directions, it's time to start walking around your dog. Like the previous step, each step requires a 10/10 success before you go to the following step.

When you start to walk counterclockwise around your dog (rewarding each step at the beginning of this process), you may notice your dog break position regularly; if so, make sure, with leash pressure, to put your dog in the original place you issued the down. Dogs like to keep their eye on their handler while walking around them, so it may be difficult for your dog to watch you walking around and turning their head to the opposite side to keep tracking. When you see your dog make this decision, jackpot and release.

Now that you have used food to communicate what you want from the DOWN command to your dog, you can start rewarding with a ball or tug (only on a long lead or short lead lost on the ground in a controlled environment). Remember that your marker for the ball/tug is a release command, so as soon as you want to reward, it is the end of that command repetition. Ensure your ball/tug is hidden when issuing commands (back pocket, in a jumper or stuffed in your pants) so your dog reliably follows verbal commands. When rewarding your dog with the ball/tug, make sure you mark before reaching for the ball and throwing it or tugging and playing the game. This is only used for dogs that find value in these games, don't force your dog to like the ball or tug if they show no interest.

If your dog is into playing FETCH, it is an excellent opportunity to develop impulse control by teaching your dog to do passive behaviours for active and high-drive rewards. While your dog is in the drive for the ball, it may be a little more challenging to have your dog comply. Be patient, stay consistent and always finish on a positive note to look after the energy for the next session. A jackpot for the ball or tug is multiple throws or multiple games of tug where your dog wins the game from time to time. Only reward with a ball/tug where appropriate and safe, as it's not practical to throw a ball at a coffee shop or close to a busy road, but also remember that the reward you give your dog will influence their state of mind. For most dogs, food reward will elicit a calmer state of mind compared to the ball/tug.

Walking around your dog is essential for practicality later in the training as you will require your dog to stay in the DOWN while you walk away out of sight—having enough impulse control to remain in the DOWN position while other dogs or interesting things are in your dog's presence. To improve the 3 D's, you will need to set goals for you and your dog, e.g., 5 minutes while you walk in different directions on the long lead in the front yard of your house/property, to begin with. Increasing duration and distance come hand in hand at this stage of the process, and controlling where you train will allow you to introduce different distractions (dog walking across the road, birds landing close by, cars making sounds or people walking by the house). If your dog breaks position before release command, offer a 'NO' plus leash pressure to correct your dog.

As you both become competent and confident with this level, practising in many different environments and while walking your dog is essential. DOWN is quite a necessary and advantageous behaviour to train your dog to do as it allows you to keep your dog in position for an extended period while in a fixed state and relaxed.

If you are in a higher distraction environment and your DOWN is now becoming more reliable but still in progress, after issuing a command, and your dog is lying down next to you, place your heel on the leash so if your dog goes to stand up, immediately as your dog breaks position will feel leash pressure and will automatically lay down through conditioning of the downward leash pressure.

While in training sessions, start to chain behaviours together in a non-specific pattern. From the SIT, issue the command DOWN; from SIT, walk away and issue COME. After your dog comes to you, give the DOWN command and reward from there and so on. Don't become too predictable about issuing the DOWN command to improve reliability and clarity.

Implementing the DOWN while walking would be an additional step in your training routine. While walking, slow down but do not stop; say 'DOWN' and gesture to the ground. You may need to add slight leash pressure. Training your dog to DOWN on command while you are moving can be challenging, so practise this at a plodding pace and increase your speed as your dog understands that they must DOWN while you're in motion. After taking a few steps away, you will reward with either food, a ball or a tug.

Another method of introducing movement to the DOWN command is moving on the spot while issuing the DOWN command. While your dog is accustomed to your feet moving while giving the command, begin to move around while your feet move on the spot to show your dog that the DOWN command may be issued while walking and in motion, not only in a static position.

Because of your intermittent reward schedule for successful repetitions and correction for non-compliance (breaking before being released), you will notice that this command is becoming more robust, more reliable, and fun. Your dog will understand that this is a way of life and communication that allows you to use it when needed. Ensure you don't overwhelm your dog by doing too many repetitions or progressing to an environment that is too busy. If this is a regular occurrence, you will hinder the reliability of command and likely stress out you and your dog.

A final step of training the DOWN command is to go to a local coffee shop or park bench and tether your lead to a fixed anchor point (strong table or post). Sit on the chair or bench and tell your dog to 'DOWN'. Reward for reasonable efforts depending on what's happening around you and make sure your dog stays DOWN until you release. Release your dog before they break position and remember how long your dog can hold the DOWN position (release before you go too long). Go for a quick stroll or pee break and come back to your seating and repeat the process.

Once your dog can hold the DOWN and be relaxed for 10 minutes, it is time for you to walk away (at an appropriate distance and duration at your dog's level) while being tethered for safety. If your dog breaks, walk back and correct your dog via leash pressure. If you are a few metres away and see your dog break position, and you issue verbal correction ('UH-UH'), you may notice your dog lay down, meaning you don't need to walk up and follow through. You must follow through with leash pressure if your dog ignores verbal correction.

Over a few weeks or months' progress, you should start to walk away, out of sight from your dog, to ensure that they stay in the DOWN while you are not present. This will allow you to progress to the Proofing phase of the DOWN. Use the following steps:

- Have your treat pouch full of tasty food.

- With NO food in your hand, say 'DOWN' and make the gesture (hand moves to the ground).

- As soon as your dog lays down, say 'YES' and reward.

- Move from a familiar environment (inside your house/backyard) to where there are more distractions (move to the front yard, footpath, park, etc.) Reward intermittently or for the excellent DOWNS.

- Say 'DOWN' and point to the ground. As soon as your dog lays down, slowly stand up, back straight, 'YES', and reward.

- If your dog knows the command and chooses not to perform the behaviour, ensure they are not overwhelmed with too many things happening around them. If this is the case, you have gone too far.

- If your dog chooses not to 'DOWN', apply gentle yet consistent pressure on the lead down at the same time as saying 'DOWN'. When your dog lays down, remove the pressure, 'YES' + REWARD.

- Remember to jackpot the best attempts, even if you need to apply pressure or not on other occasions.

- On the other hand, only reward sometimes, so your dog learns to do the command without being rewarded.

Training DOWN leash pressure introduction as correction 1

https://me-qr.com/FqPzKdAV

Training DOWN leash pressure introduction as correction 2

https://me-qr.com/VVIihXyd

Proofing 'DOWN'

Remember that what you choose to achieve in your dog training is up to you and your goals. Dog needs will vary from family to family. To proof any command reflects your expectations, experience level, amount of time you invest, and what is practical for your life.

For example, as a dog trainer, I need the following:

- I need my dog to be able to hold a very long down stay (up to half an hour) while out of sight at times and while other dogs and worldly distractions present themselves. My dog needs to be able to do this off lead while I am working with clients and their dogs, and my dog may need to wait whether it is in the front yard of a client's house, at a local park or busy intersection until I release him out of position.

- I need my dogs to stay in a DOWN while reactive dogs bark at them, people walk up to them, and all other distractions pass by. I need my dogs to be able to DOWN on command while they are walking or running next to me and hold it until I release them or to hold their DOWN while I play with my son in the playground while he is 30 m from me.

This is my lifestyle, and I train my dogs to be able to comply until I have a proofed command. I heavily manage my dogs to set them up for success in every way possible.

Generalising the DOWN command in every environment where you spend regular time with your dog is the most important part of proofing this command. You never totally stop rewarding your dog in the proofing phase, but you certainly need to build up to a point where your dog does not need to be rewarded for maintaining this behaviour. This means that your dog fully understands what the command is, and you must reward less in this phase. Otherwise, you are not proofing the command. The reward is a potential, not a guarantee. On the other hand, correction is guaranteed if your dog chooses not to follow the command or prematurely breaks position, and this gives your dog a level of motivation to commit to the behaviour (potentially earn reinforcement and avoid punishment).

Techniques to further proof the DOWN command would be to issue a DOWN command while walking at an average pace and add necessary duration, distance and distraction. At an appropriate distance, recall your dog (discussed in the next section). As your dog is running toward you, issue the DOWN command.

For dogs that like to chase the ball, throw the ball; as your dog runs to retrieve the ball, issue the DOWN command. When your dog DOWNS on the way to the ball, give the marker for the ball 'FETCH', and your dog will be reinforced and continue to retrieve the ball.

We want to ensure our dog will be DOWN in all circumstances. These techniques help proof the command as we are telling our dog to stop moving while in a high-drive state of mind, which will reflect a situation where your dog is to chase something or is to run towards an undesirable situation and that you can ensure you can stop your dog by issuing the DOWN command.

These suggestions in the proofed section are general because it's challenging to explain specifics. Be sure to know your training goals and what you expect, need, and want your dog to perform as a final behaviour and in what circumstance.

These steps should guide you to think so that you can continue to work on behaviours over a long-term basis and equip you with ideas to adapt to your lifestyle, routine, and way of life with your dog.

Teaching the recall 'COME'

The recall is one of the most important commands you will teach your dog, being potentially lifesaving! To be sure you are clear to your dog from the beginning, you need to understand what the word 'COME' should mean to your dog. Before teaching this command, we want to make sure it is understood from the beginning that the word 'COME' means a dog runs to you and automatically sits at your feet within arm's reach and remains in position until being released.

Your dog must know that the recall means sitting at your feet for a few fundamental reasons. You do not want your dog to run full speed at you and run into you, causing injury. You also do not want your dog to run full speed in your direction only to run past you, which loses its function.

I want you to teach your dog that when you issue the command 'COME', they end up sitting at your feet so that you can grab hold of your dog's collar to secure them by attaching a leash, grab the collar to bring your dog inside or to have your dog to come to you and not run away immediately after sitting or feeding some food.

The point of the recall is to have your dog come to you and wait for further instruction, whether to secure him, issue another command, or let them return to what they were doing in their free time. I only let my dogs off the lead entirely if they have reliable RECALL and DOWN commands. We must understand that we should teach these practical and functional commands before teaching tricks or giving any dog too much freedom in an unsecured environment.

Step 1

In your backyard, courtyard or inside your house (distraction-free environment), attach your dog to lead/collar and have food in a treat pouch. In Step 1, we have our dog on the left-hand side and have you and your dog face the same direction for this process. Let your dog know you have food in your hand by letting them smell your closed fist with food, start walking in a straight line, and remember to walk facing one direction.

Watch the video on this QR code as a visual example of this step of the recall command.

https://me-qr.com/3qx6MXA6

Say 'COME' and start walking semi-fast backwards with your lure hand in front of your dog's nose and your knees. After taking approximately five steps backwards, stop and lift your hand from your knees to your chest while standing back straight (this should allow your dog to automatically sit without you having to say SIT). As soon as your dog's butt touches the ground, MARK + REWARD. If you say SIT and reward, you are now rewarding the SIT, not 'COME'. Remember, 'COME' means a dog running to you and sitting at your feet.

The lure hand is essential to get correct from the beginning—hand in front of knees. If your hand drifts off to either the left or right side of your body, your dog will likely be next to you, run behind you, and get messy. Another reason for the lure hand to be clearly in front of your knees is that when you stop and lift your hand to your chest, that motion will allow your dog to sit without giving a verbal command. Finally, the lure hand in front of your knees becomes the non-verbal gesture representing the RECALL. Remember, we issue verbal command ('COME'), and we have non-verbal command (hand in the line of your knees). Both should give the same result (the dog runs to you in a straight line and sits at your feet). When you're ready, release your dog and repeat STAGE 1 of RECALL 3-5 times and ensure you finish on a positive note.

In the first stages of this command, I recommend rewarding multiple times while your dog is holding the sit position. This will help you keep your dog in front of you, anticipating numerous separate rewards. Otherwise, your dog may take the food, assume no more rewards will be delivered, and run away from you. Do this by marking 'YES', bending over to feed, standing back straight, and 'YES' again and bending over to feed. Purposefully straightening back between each reward is important because if you only straighten your back before 'OK' and releasing, then your dog will assume standing straight is a cue to be released.

After a few days of the above practice, the next step is to test if your dog understands the command and gesture. Walk your dog around your backyard, as they are at the end of the leash, and say your dog's name as soon as your dog looks at you; in this sequence, say 'COME' immediately after verbal command, issue the gesture (hand in front of your knees) and when your dog runs to you, lift your hand to chest and reward for sit position. This is the same process as step one. However, we are standing in one spot and not running backwards. If your dog is struggling and doesn't understand what to do after you say 'COME' and give a gesture, start moving back, which may trigger your dog to come closer to you.

Only reward when your dog is within arms' reach of you. Otherwise, your dog will practice sitting 1 m from you, which will develop into a habit and will work against you in the long term. We want to be able to hold onto their collar after the recall and not run away.

Before moving to STAGE 2 of RECALL, you want to condition your dog as part of the teaching phase, which will require us to briefly hold your dog's collar while they are sitting at your feet. Call your dog to 'COME' when your dog sits at your feet, before rewarding, briefly touch the collar and mark 'YES' + FOOD. If your dog breaks position when you touch their collar, do not feed. Repeat the RECALL process to show your dog what he should do to receive a reward. You need to be able to handle your dog's collar. This will teach your dog that touching the collar is a part of the process and is tolerable and encouraging when you try to get a hold of their collar. If we do not teach this early on, we risk making your dog concerned when you get a hold of your dog's collar, which can have undesirable and even dangerous consequences.

If the only time you get a hold of your dog's collar is when you need to gain control, your dog may duck, weave and run away from you to escape the reprimand. Usually, when we decide our dog is 'out of control', it is when they are over-excited or over-aroused in the presence of certain stimuli (people, dogs, or other animals). Holding their collar is a way to stop them from engaging in a very exciting thing.

Ideally, you should be able to get a hold of your dog's collar without conflict. Practice it when you do not need it, so when you need to, you can get a hold of your dog without the silly games. Even better, you want your dog to want you to get a hold of their collar in anticipation of a potential reward. At worst, your dog will not fight you when you go to hold their collar. Remember that these essential and functional commands must have practical use in all circumstances in an effort to ensure your dog's safety, improve your relationship, and have processes in place to keep our experiences in and outside of the home desirable.

Step 2

The main point of step two is to practice RECALL off the lead in our home, introducing multiple people and make a game out of the command. Wait until your dog performs step one 10/10 times successfully in a row before you start STEP 2.

In the backyard of your home (or secure distraction-free area) with two or more people, make a circle or be spaced 5 m apart around your dog. Make sure everyone has food in their hand. Have one person at a time say your dog's name, and as soon as your dog looks, say 'COME' and have your hand in front of your knees.

There is no movement from people at this stage; everyone is standing in the same spot. Repeat in a different pattern so your dog doesn't pick up on the sequence that each person will predictably call them.

In this stage, reward every time, to begin with. Ensure that rewards only come to your dog when they sit at your feet and are randomly touched on the collar. Remember to release your dog ('OK') to break the sit.

After 5-10 successful repetitions, everyone steps back to increase the distance between people and dogs. Over a few days, as this game is practised, space out throughout the house/backyard so that your dog cannot see the person calling. If they hear their name followed by command and come to find you and sit at your feet, you are approaching the training phase of the RECALL.

When your dog does this 10/10 in a row, start to reward intermittently so that they are not getting a reward every single time, but on the random and best efforts. You can do this stage on your own. Make sure your dog is a few meters away from you and is not looking at you when you are calling your dog to come.

Training RECALL

When your dog clearly and reliably understands the RECALL command inside the boundaries of your home, free of distraction, you are ready to proceed to the next phase—the training phase. Make sure you have a 10 m nylon lead attached to your dog's collar and move to the front yard (or to a mildly busy environment) close to your property where there are some distractions. Your dog should have other things to pay attention to but not overly distracted where they cannot focus on you.

While your dog is approximately 5 m from you, say their name. As soon as your dog looks at you, call them to 'COME' and ensure, as always, that your dog is sitting at your feet before rewarding him. Remember to reward intermittently and jackpot the best efforts if your dog leaves distraction (a smell or another dog across the road). If your dog is ignoring you, apply pressure on the long lead and say their name; as soon as they look at you, say 'COME' as your dog starts moving towards you, and release the pressure and reward as they approach you. Sometimes we will MARK + REWARD for the dog approaching to keep their motivation level high, and then we can increase the criteria by rewarding them when they sit at your feet in future repetitions. Remember to set your dog up for success and keep early training sessions short and sweet to ensure your dog loves and understands the game.

If you know your dog can perform the RECALL but has chosen to ignore you, hand over hand, pull the long lead towards you to make your dog come into position. The consequence for non-compliance is a correction where we must educate your dog that if you issue the command, they MUST come. If your dog is ignoring you completely, only give the command 'COME' after you have repeated their name a few times and have your dog's attention on you. It is preferable to repeat their name and only give formal commands ONCE rather than saying your dog's name once and repeating the command over and over.

If you are only starting this process, only recall your dog if you have food handy and make sure you can follow through and make your dog come back (leash pressure). Also, ensure that your dog is capable of performing the behaviour in the environment you are in.

If you want your dog to come close to you, but you're in a very highly distracting situation, it is best to give an informal command ('HERE') than to provide the formal command'COME'. This will ensure you do not ruin the formal command (running straight to you and sitting at your feet). I find that the word 'COME' may be overused or misused, telling your dog to come to you in an over stimulating environment setting them up for failure. Using an informal command like 'HERE' will help prevent watering down your formal RECALL ('COME').

A common mistake owners make is asking too much of their dog too soon, which can taint the command as we tend to get frustrated or the dog needs clarification. If you practice in the front yard for a day or two, and the next time you attempt the RECALL is when your dog is playing with another dog in the park, you're setting yourself and your dog up for failure. Going from step 5 to step 20 overnight is a way to untrain the behaviour you intend to teach. Taking your time for longevity and reliability is critical. The 3 P's (Practice, Patience, Persistence) are to be remembered at this level of the command.

Proceeding to the next step of incorporating more distractions and busier environments will take a few weeks to months of daily practice. Take the initiative to practice randomly on the walk (short lead) when your dog sees something appealing in the distance. Set your dog up for success and find as many different situations as possible in which you can drill this command before moving to the next step.

Every walk consists of following the 20/20/20 rule (refer to 'The Walk' section) in the middle of the walk when we give our dog free time on the long lead. At the park is where we can start training the RECALL along with other commands that are in the 'training phase'. As you walk through the park, practice RECALL when there are no competing distractions around you. While in the park, you can reward your dog with the ball/tug if it is something your dog finds more rewarding than food. Remember to reward intermittently, not every single time, and make it fun and engaging for you and your dog.

While your dog is playing with another dog, it is an excellent opportunity to RECALL while they are in play mode. Make a big fun reward event or allow them to go back and continue playing with the other dog. For many reasons, this allows your dog to practice impulse control to stop high-level activities instead of ignoring your command and returning to you.

To ensure you're the most important thing in your dog's life, you must be able to practice exercises like this to control your dog's experiences. What if the play has gone too far? RECALL your dog. What if the person doesn't want to be jumped on by your dog? RECALL your dog. What if your dog is running towards the road or into the mouth of an aggressive dog? RECALL your dog.

It is good to start implementing the RECALL while you are slightly out of sight. You can do this while you are walking through parklands and you have your dog attached to a long lead. Whether you are holding the lead or letting it loose on the ground always ensure your dog is safe from running onto a road, running up to other dogs/people or running away from you.

Whether behind a toilet block, behind shrubs or a tree, around the corner of a wall, etc., ensure the lead is within arm's reach so that if your dog chooses not to come, you immediately reel them in.

It's important to pressure test the recall in as many different scenarios, environments, and situations that your dog will likely experience so that we can start to proof this command to be a reliable behaviour that we can depend on.

As time passes and you are consistent with this practice, many things will present themselves (people, animals, and things) that your dog wants to run up to.

If it is inappropriate to approach the thing, RECALL your dog. If your dog chooses not to come, reel in the leash to show your dog that they must comply. If your dog decides to come to you, make a big fun game and sometimes only praise him.

Intermittently getting a hold of your dog's collar when in these situations is most important in case one day your dog slips the collar, the lead slips out of your hands, or your dog runs out of the car when you open the door when you

RECALL him. You should always be able to get a firm hold of the collar to either attach a lead, pick them up or put your dog back in the car, etc.

Move from a familiar environment (inside your house/backyard) to where there are more distractions For example, gradually move to the front yard, footpath, park, etc.

Here's how:

- Attach your dog to a long lead.

- Have high-value food handy.

- Call your dog's name for attention, say 'COME', and proceed to have your hand on your knee.

- Your dog will run up to you, lift your hand to gesture to sit, MARK + reward.

- Start rewarding intermittently.

- Lots of praise and jackpot when your dog leaves a distraction (another dog or a smell they are fixated on) and comes to you.

- If your dog is ignoring you, apply pressure on the long lead and say their name; as soon as they look at you, say 'COME'. As your dog starts moving towards you, release the pressure and reward as they approach you.

- Only say 'COME' once your dog has attention on you. Otherwise, your dog will lose the value of the word COME if you say it too many times without the behaviour following.

Training RECALL- Step 2

https://me-qr.com/3qx6MXA6

Training RECALL- Using jackpot and intermittent reward

https://me-qr.com/CoBshvKg

Proofing RECALL

Remember that what you choose to achieve in your dog training is up to you and your goals since needs vary from owner to owner. How you proof any command will reflect your expectations, experience level, amount of time you invest, and what is practical for your life.

I need all my dogs to RECALL by coming every time I call them and to wait at my feet, within arm's reach, until I release, attach a leash, or issue another command (e.g., DOWN). I need this for safety, practicality, duty, and respect for the community/surroundings we are in and to maintain a calm and enjoyable outing with my dogs. When proofing RECALL, ensure you are in a safe and appropriate environment and do not let your dog have a level of freedom they are not ready for.

The RECALL in this phase should be a behaviour your dog performs 100% of the time under all circumstances and at any level of drive your dog is in. Through hundreds of repetitions of training the RECALL, we should be able to walk through a 1000-acre private property with your dog off the leash. We use our RECALL not as a game or training session, it should be a language you speak to ensure your communication is of the highest form.

As you walk through this hypothetical property, you will encounter many things, especially wild animals. If you notice your dog chasing a rabbit, your RECALL should be compelling enough for your dog to leave the rabbit and return to you. In an example like this, your dog should come to you because they think a high-value reward will come, such as a ball/tug or food. Your dog should also consider that if they don't COME, you will issue correction (via leash pressure or leash pop). You can see this is a high level many people do not reach. If you have yet to train to get to this point, management must consistently be implemented. Walk through the property with your dog on a long lead. Otherwise, your dog may want to avoid coming as they chase the rabbit and may find themselves stuck in a barbed wire fence, lost over the hill, or many other unforeseen consequences.

To proof your RECALL takes years of training along with consistent and mindful interactions. Your dog should be able to play/interact with other dogs and come to you as soon as you issue the RECALL. Your dog should be able to RECALL even after throwing the ball, as it may be a situation where your dog is in danger (after throwing the ball, it may bounce off your dog's nose onto the road).

Ensure you have an informal recall, e.g., 'HERE', meaning loosely come close to me, as you may use this in lower-level circumstances and not have to reward it so mindfully. Most people will not get a proofed RECALL as they issue the 'COME' (formal command) too often and do not reinforce it often enough or follow through if the dog chooses to check out. It is important that your dog is super motivated to come when called, as it should be a super reliable command, especially if you wish to enjoy off-leash times with your dog.

The 'BED' command

The 'BED' command is another essential command as a part of your training. It is the most used command inside your house; however, it can be used in many different applications and scenarios.

The 'BED'command is called a placement command, which means we should be able to send our dog to a specific location (e.g., a bed, towel, blanket or item on the ground) and stay there until it is released. This becomes especially necessary inside your home as it is less practical to call your dog to COME or DOWN when inside the house and much more beneficial to send them to their place until told to be released.

The most common applications of this command are when visitors come over, when the family is enjoying dinner, when our dog wants to run amuck inside your home, or when out and about, sending your dog to a specific spot may be very beneficial.

Here are a few examples of the 'BED' command:

- When family friends visited, Mia, a four-year-old little girl, walked through the door. Nuki, our Maltese/Pomeranian, excitedly approached Mia to greet her. It was apparent that Mia was uncomfortable with Nuki enthusiastically tap dancing (almost jumping on Mia). I told Nuki to go to her BED (no food or lead). Nuki stayed in her BED for 5 minutes until I released her, and she calmly approached Mia and Nuki received some calm, loving pats.

- When I visit the Vet and need to weigh my dog, I issue the 'BED'command, and my dog will lay on the scales to be weighed. Otherwise, I need to force my dog on a slippery surface in an environment filled with stress hormones, which may be a conflicting experience for any dog.

- As we set up a picnic area for family and babies, dogs sniffed and walked around off lead. I set up two towels 7 m from our picnic blanket under the tree. When it was time for us all to sit and enjoy lunch, I whistled to my dogs for their attention and issued the 'BED' command. The dogs walked straight to their towel and lay there (off lead, no rewards) until I released them 1 hour later for us to stretch our legs, throw the ball, etc.

As you can see, once we proof this command, it holds some powerful functions.

I enjoy my dogs in many situations with ease because I can have a level of control over my them, which means in the long term, they get to experience more things safely and calmly, while gaining more love and respect from the ones around them.

Furthermore, most people are so focused on telling their dogs what NOT to do, instead of focusing more on what we want them to do. It is hard to jump on four-year-old Mia while on the bed 5 m away.

Stress reduces and dogs are more confident when told to lay on the scales rather than be physically forced, and it's hard to steal food or step on babies on a picnic blanket if the dogs are on their bed 7 m away waiting to be released. If you take the time to be specific to your dog, your return on investment will be greater as life rolls on.

Teaching 'BED'

Start by having a dog bed that your dog can easily walk and lay on inside the house with no distractions. Have a treat pouch filled with high-value food and have your dog's full attention. Lure your dog onto the BED. As soon as all four paws touch the BED, immediately MARK + REWARD multiple times to reinforce being on the bed. To release your dog off the BED, say 'OK' and feeding away from the BED. Repeat the above step, if your dog breaks as soon as you reward, lure them back on and continue to reward while on the bed.

Once you can easily lure your dog onto the bed, reward multiple times for staying on the bed (up to 10 seconds), try to straighten your back between every reward to show your dog that you standing straight up is not the end but a continuation. Expecting another reward as you stand straight. Always say 'OK' before offering food away from the bed for your dog to be released off the BED.

Once you can lure your dog onto the bed 10/10 with all four paws touching the bed, you are ready to introduce the verbal command 'BED'. When your dog is off the bed looking at you, say the word 'BED', and a second later, lure your dog onto the bed. MARK + REWARD each time, stand up straight, and increase the duration by waiting an extra second between each reward to encourage your dog to stay on the BED before you release. If your dog breaks before the release, say 'NO' (verbal non-reward marker) and repeat the above process.

As your dog can stay on the bed for up to 10 seconds 10/10 times in a row, you can now take a tiny step away from the bed after standing straight between each reward and before releasing. Make sure you take this single step in different directions each time (one to the left, one to the right and a backward step) to make sure your dog doesn't only see you stepping in one direction and anticipate the release command.

In this stage of the command, we want to achieve 1 minute of BED while you can walk a circle around your dog while staying on the BED. Only introduce an extra step once your dog can remain on the bed 10/10 from the number of steps you can take (if you can do three steps from your dog but breaks frequently, do not add a fourth step until your dog knows to wait for release at three steps).

Before proceeding to the training phase of this command, you want to ensure that your dog understands that the command 'BED' is followed by the hand lure (pointing to the BED), which means stay on BED until hearing the release command ('OK') after you can walk a circle around the bed.

Remember to randomly reward the release command after saying 'OK', as sometimes you may notice your dog staying on the bed, figuring they get more rewards by staying on the bed. Do not reward every release, sometimes praise or merely being released off the bed is rewarding enough for some dogs.

- Lure your dog to their bed
- As soon as all four paws touch the bed, say 'BED' + 'YES' and reward
- Reward multiple times for staying on the bed
- Lure your dog off the bed and say, 'OK'. Once the dog gets off the bed, reward and repeat this process

Teaching 'BED' command

https://me-qr.com/vIYEi1ns

Training 'BED'

In this phase of the 'BED' command, we introduce intermittent rewards and leash pressure correction for breaking early or not going to BED on command. Having a leash attached sets you and your dog up for success, ensuring you can effectively control your dog and help them to be clear of your expectations.

Have a bed within 1 m from you. Say your dog's name, as soon as your dog looks at you, say 'BED'. One second later, give a gesture by pointing to the bed (no food in your hand). As soon as your dog goes to the BED, wait 2 seconds before MARK + REWARD. Before releasing, take a step away from your dog and wait 1 second before rewarding. If they break as you increase duration and distance, apply leash pressure (2/10) towards the BED. As soon as your dog gets back on the bed, take a step back for one second before rewarding him. Keep repeating this step for 3-4 repetitions before ending the session. If your dog keeps breaking position, try taking a smaller step or just moving one foot before rewarding.

Remember, having the leash on sometimes confuses your

dog, and it may tend to follow you. Do not apply pressure on lead when stepping away. Therefore, attaching the leash to the dog for training sessions is essential as it becomes a reliable cue that you and your dog will be doing fun stuff together via training, playing, and, of course, walking.

If the lead only represents the walk, your dog will lose their mind with excitement seeing the leash, hindering your training session. Having no leash attached in this process makes it difficult and conflicting because when your dog breaks the position too early, you have less control to put them back on the BED, which causes frustration and confusion.

When your dog breaks the 'BED' command early, do not repeat the command 'BED', instead, give verbal correction, and apply pressure. If you re-issue a command after breaking, your dog will anticipate a reward, so in turn, breaking a position may become reinforced as a command will follow. If we give the marker ('UH-UH') before pressure, it further supports that the command 'BED' means stay on the bed until being released or been issued another command.

Once you achieve 10/10 success with 1 step, continue to walk around the BED as per the previous practice in the teaching phase. Now with your dog understanding that they must stay on the bed, begin to change the sequence of where the bed is located (different spots in the house and backyard). When walking away, switch between clockwise and counter-clockwise; do different speeds and types of steps, and increase duration, working towards 1 min. Here you are increasing DURATION, and DISTANCE, and generalising the command to show your dog that it is not a geographic location that matters but rather the BED you want your dog to go on.

As part of the training phase, you must implement different 'BEDS' such as using a towel, blanket, t-shirt, doormat, etc. This act generalises the command further and means lying and staying in a place that has a different texture to the ground. Doing this will help with the function of the command by making it more practical for many areas of daily life (e.g. at the park, at a friend's house, the vet, and so on).

You will be ready for the next step once your dog has achieved a 1-minute duration on the bed while you can walk around your dog and take a minimum of 5 steps away without breaking.

Once you are confident that your dog is focused on you and the training, it is time to continue training outside the house, in the driveway, in the front yard, and even on the footpath in front of your home (depending on how much stimulus is around you).

You will notice your dog will be less engaged and focused on you as moving outside presents a range of distractions you need to work through. Working on the 3 D's incrementally together as Duration and Distraction need to be increased before making too much Distance when moving to a busier environment.

Just like with all your training, you must be clear about your goals and what you want your dog to do specifically. With the 'BED' command, you must write down clearly how long you want your dog to stay on their BED and how far you want to be able to walk away from them while they remain on the bed.

What environment will you expect your dog to stay on BED for a set duration? These are important to refine and continuously consider, as every single training session is a step closer to your specific goals and expectations. If you are a personal trainer and wish to bring your dog to work with you, then your goals would something like:

- Duration: 45 min

- Distance: 10 m

- Distraction: People jumping up and down, dogs, birds, sounds, etc.

If you want your dog to be calm when the kid's friends come over, the 'BED' command would be 10 m with kids running around while you're within the house. If you know exactly what you are training for, it is more likely your dog will begin to understand what is expected of him.

While training the 'BED' command, you should start chaining commands together in the front yard and with your dog on a long lead. While they are sniffing around, issue the commands in this order:

1. RECALL, DOWN, BED, walk away, and then proceed to reward your dog before releasing.

2. Make sure you mix the sequence of your commands, durations, and when you reward,

becoming predictably unpredictable so that your commands are not always the same. When the training location changes, your 3 Ds also change.

3. Remember to jackpot your dog's best efforts and always finish training sessions on a positive note!

As you progress with this training, it is time to start sending your dog to the bed from further distances away from the bed. Begin with 1 m and, then over time, increase the distance once your dog understands it is the bed they are supposed to go to. You may sometimes notice that when you issue the verbal command 'BED' your dog will just look at you, proceed to point and walk toward BED, or use spatial pressure (walking into your dog's space) to help correct them by getting onto the bed yourself. Always ensure the verbal command comes one second before the gesture to train your dog that the verbal command will announce the gesture, so over time, you will not need to point. Your verbal command should be clear enough with effective timing and consistency.

Include many types of distractions inside the house: a doorbell, door knock, people dancing, playing, food on the coffee table, etc. It would be best to generalise as much as possible to effectively communicate and control your dog in the event visitors come over. Practice when you do not need it, so when you do, it's a skill that can be used when you need it.

- With no food in your hand, point to the bed (stay close to the bed at first) and say 'BED'. As soon as your dog is on the bed, stand up straight and say 'YES' +

REWARD.

- Start moving away from the bed one step at a time and say 'BED' followed by your gesture. When your dog goes onto the bed, say 'YES' and reward.

- Move to unfamiliar areas around the house and change the material of the bed (use a towel, different beds, etc.) to generalise the behaviour so your dog understands to do this behaviour for different beds in different places.

- If your dog chooses not to perform the known command, attach a lead to its collar and apply gentle pressure toward the bed 1 second after saying 'BED'. Once the dog gets on the bed, offer 'YES' + REWARD.

- Start sending your dog to the bed from further distances. Start with 1 m and incrementally (with 10/10 success) add an extra meter of distance.

- Also, start increasing how long your dog can stay on the bed until being released. Start by staying close by to guide your dog with the collar back to the bed if it breaks before releasing.

- Increase your distance from your dog while they are on the bed. Do not go too far too quickly. Make it a steady and incremental distance so that it is clear to your dog that they must stay before being released.

- This must also be practised with new distractors (e.g., visitors, other dogs, or sounds your dog reacts to).

- The 3 D's of DISTANCE, DURATION & DISTRACTION, are essential to improving this command.

Training 'BED' command

https://me-qr.com/A63Jsf6J

Proofing 'BED'

When training regularly and daily toward your goal, the 'BED' command will transition into the proofed phase. Tell your dog 'BED' with no gesture, food, or leash pressure.

When your dog remains for the required duration, distance, and distractions in many environments until released, you'll know if you have a proofed command. The 'BED' command is an essential command that holds a superior function and develops solid impulse control.

Begin by sending your dog to the BED from further distances, even if the BED is in another room. In this phase, your dog will realise that being released from the BED becomes rewarding as it will give your dog access to your visitors or to what is appropriate.

Use the 'BED' command to check your dog's weight at the vet, offer a safe place to rest while setting up a campsite/park, and to have a reliable command in the home.

You should always adhere to the rules, remember to release your dog from the BED, and follow through if your dog does not comply.

Rewarding in the proofed phase is still necessary; however, it should be less frequent and under more difficult circumstances.

Telling your dog to go to bed will become the language and communication you share with your dog. It should represent a calm and reliable place for your dog without conflict or confusion.

Remember, proofed behaviours are a manifestation of solid training and a reflection of your way of life with your dog. You get what you reward. Your dog's habits are an extension of your habits, and what is a habit will become an element of our character, both dog and owner.

- Once your dog reliably goes to bed on command, you must be sure to reward variably and intermittently to keep the command strong.

- You should be able to send your dog to the bed from a longer distance away (from one room to another) or when the doorbell rings.

- If your dog breaks position before releasing, you must follow it up by using pressure on the collar or spacial pressure to communicate that they must stay until released.

- Use your release command instead of food to

reinforce behaviour, especially if you have a friend over and the dog wants to go and say hello. This becomes rewarding to the dog because they have understood that staying on the bed will grant them access to what they wish—only when it is under your command and your dog is in a settled state of mind.

- When you are in the proofed phase, you will know when you can send your dog to a bed (towel, t-shirt, scales at the vet, anything that is a different texture to the ground) when in new environments.

- Your dog should be able to stay there until released for a longer duration than you have decided to be appropriate. (REFER TO 'BED IN FUNCTION')

The 'LOOK' Command

The function of the LOOK command is to have a verbal command for your dog to look and stare at you immediately. This command is used for many reasons, one of which is an integral part of working through reactive behaviour from your dog. If you can effectively have your dog focus on you on cue, you can successfully begin ' to desensitise your dog to certain stimuli. The word LOOK is staring at you until rewarded or released. Their name, on the other hand, is a cue to check in and gain your dog's attention, which is an important distinction. Another way of explaining it is that LOOK is a behaviour we wish to teach, and your dog's NAME is to have your dog engaging with you (a mindset).

It is essential to have a dog that focuses on you, especially in public, where there are so many external stimuli that your dog wants to engage with or feels threatened and wants the thing to go away. Giving a command to say 'focus on me' is a helpful way to create a neutral dog (not overly concerned with everyday things) and a dog that looks to you for instruction, attention, and guidance.

Teaching 'LOOK'

- With food in your hand, lure your hand to the side of your face. As soon as your dog looks into your eyes, MARK + reward. Say 'LOOK' one second before luring.

- Practice this while your dog is on lead and in a SIT on your left-hand side. Use your right hand to lure from the dog's nose to your right ear.

- Hold the LOOK for 1 second before rewarding.

- Once you can say, 'LOOK' and your dog looks at you without the lure ten times out of ten in a row, you can proceed to the training phase.

Training 'LOOK'

- Once your dog is looking at you on command, you must reward the behaviour intermittently. If your dog is struggling, help them by using a hand gesture. After saying 'LOOK', gesture your empty hand to your ear, when your dog looks at you, wait for two seconds before rewarding. Remember, no luring (food in your hand) for this training phase. Say 'LOOK' when your dog looks at you, 'YES', and then reach to your pouch to give the reward. For the repetitions you do not reward, either say 'OK' to release out of the behaviour or praise your dog.

- Adding a light 1/10 tap on the lead before issuing the verbal command will help prime your dog to look at you as a result of the tap on the lead and will help when your dog needs extra assistance to LOOK rather than being outwardly focused on something else. The tap prior to LOOK will also become a conditioned cue. Usually, tightening the leash will cause your dog to push against the lead and react. Counter condition leash pressure to become a cue to focus on you and not react. This will take lots of practice and precise timing; however, you can achieve this, and it will become beneficial in your training application.

- Move from inside your house to the front yard or footpath in front of your home. Practice the LOOK command while your dog looks at something in the distance. For mild distractions, offer praise or release; medium-level distractions a reward; and jackpot high distracting stimuli.

- Jackpot when your dog LOOKS and hold the LOOK for a longer duration. Start with your dog looking at you for one second, then extend the duration to 2, 3 and 5 seconds.

- Try your LOOK command while walking so your dog can focus on you with eye contact. Doing these two things simultaneously can be tricky but beneficial for the end result and creating a reliable command. Walk slow when issuing the LOOK command, to help your dog LOOK. Otherwise, your dog will find the LOOK command challenging when walking at a regular or fast pace. Over time gradually increase your walking speed while asking your dog to LOOK.

- If your dog does not obey the LOOK command when surrounded or in the presence of any stimulus, you may be too close, , or your dog does not know what you want. If this happens, create more distance between your dog and what they are distracted by and try again. You know your dog best, so take note of their critical distance and work from there.

Using the leash to help your dog LOOK if they choose not to can be tricky. Always start with patience and low-level pressure on the lead inside your house away from any external stimuli.

Apply pressure first (1/10), then say, 'LOOK'. As soon as your dog LOOKS, release the pressure, and simultaneously MARK + REWARD. This is to show your dog that the pressure will turn off as soon as they LOOK at you.

Your dog will always want the pressure of the collar to be released, but they may not always want food. In saying this, take note of the above advice, don't ask your dog to LOOK if you are too close to the stimuli they are reacting to, and make appropriate space before training this.

For example, f you want your dog to LOOK at you while another dog is too close to where you are training,trying to use leash pressure for your dog to LOOK can cause many issues, such as creating too much stress. If trained correctly, your dog will understand that the leash pressure is a cue to check back on you.

Another variation to using leash pressure is light tapping (nagging) on the lead. Very soft and consistent taps (1/10 intensity) can help condition your dog to look at you and for your dog to remove the undesirable nagging pressure on the lead.

Over time, nagging or leash pressure is utilised for both an operant and a classically conditioned response as the nagging becomes an apparent stimulus to your dog to look at you reflexively. This means operant—consequence for not doing the behaviour (LOOK) and classical—the nagging or leash pressure will represent LOOK and will occur automatically when presented with the leash pressure.

Proofing 'LOOK'

- This command aims to get your dog to look at you as a response to a stimulus that distracts or makes your dog reactive (barking, lunging, whining, etc.).

- Over time, you will reward randomly as you give the command 'LOOK' in the presence of another stimulus (other dogs, people, animals, etc.). If no food reward is given, praise your dog. If they are in a sit command when you say 'LOOK', you can release them and continue walking.

- As a proofed command, LOOK would be used when presented with a new stimulus your dog focuses on, and you want them to focus on you. It will represent whatever you have associated the command with, either food, praise or higher-value items (ball/tug). Still, it will also have the effect, through counter conditioning, that will help your dog feel better about the stimuli present and perform the actual behaviour of LOOKING at you.

More is explained later in this book.

The TOUCH command

Teaching your dog to touch their nose to your palm is a handy and fun command with many applications. Use the TOUCH command as a practical way to position your dog, similar to luring.

For example, if you want your dog to the right-hand side of the coffee table, you say 'TOUCH', offer your hand where you want your dog to stand, and tell them to DOWN.

Adding this command to your tool kit will be handy when you least expect it and will help with future behaviours you may want to teach.

Once your dog knows the command, you can use it as a bridge to teach other commands, like how I taught my dogs to weave between my legs or to jump over things. We can use TOUCH in a chain of behaviours to increase their drive and enthusiasm for other behaviours we are training.

When I want my dog to do the new behaviour I have taught

(e.g., DOWN) with intensity and high drive, I may say, 'TOUCH' three or four times before saying 'DOWN'.

Each time you offer a known command but do not reward, you increase dopamine levels, which can help your dog do the proceeding behaviour with more intensity.

Teaching 'TOUCH'

'Have a piece of food between the base of your index and middle finger (closer to your palm, not the tips of your finger).

- Present that hand to your dog (palm facing dog's nose).

- When your dog's nose touches your hand to get the treat, 'YES' + REWARD.

- Do this with both hands.

- Once your dog does this 10 out of 10 times, start introducing the word 'TOUCH' before offering your hand. Once your dog's nose touches your hand, 'YES' + REWARD.

- Present your hand flat (NO FOOD IN HAND), palm facing your dog, and say, 'TOUCH'.

- As soon as your dog's nose touches your hand say, 'YES' + REWARD and reach to your pouch and give a treat.

- Alternate this with both hands.

Teaching TOUCH command

https://me-qr.com/vAc4UEvc

Training 'TOUCH'

- Intermittent reward is essential to introduce early, as you want to avoid your dog expecting food with every TOUCH command.

- Gradually give the TOUCH command further from your dog (start with a short distance of 30cm).

- Practice TOUCH as a way for your dog to jump onto or over objects.

- Depending on your dog's breed, age, and interest, you can offer your hand higher so they jump to TOUCH your hand.

- Start working the TOUCH command in more active environments and around distractions and jackpot the best efforts.

- Use the TOUCH command as a foundation of other commands and behaviours, such as weaving through your legs, positioning your dog in tight spots, or as a directional command.

Proofing 'TOUCH'

- Reward only randomly and for performing the behaviour under highly distracting environments.

- Using complex behaviours and trick training becomes a means of communication with your dog indirectly to do something else, which over time will be called a new command.

Leave it

The LEAVE IT' command helps control and stop your dog from eating food, picking up things in its mouth off the floor, and pursuing a specific stimulus (e.g., a cat or wildlife, for example).

When walking, your dog may approach something dangerous or inappropriate, such as a box of cooked chicken bones or a dead animal you want your dog to leave immediately.

Teaching 'LEAVE IT'

- Start by having your dog on the lead.

- Set up the scenario by putting food on the floor and having high-value treats in your pouch. You DO NOT want your dog to eat the food off the floor at any stage of this teaching/training of the 'LEAVE IT' command.

This defeats the purpose of the exercise.

- The objective is for your dog not to get into the habit of scavenging for scraps, and also, you don't want your dog to think there is any chance they can rush off to eat the food or interact with the item on the floor.

- As your dog approaches the food on the floor, say, 'LEAVE IT' and apply 2/10 pressure on the lead away from the food while walking backwards away from the food on the floor. Leash pressure is coming towards you.

- As soon as your dog moves away from the food, release the tension off the lead and MARK + REWARD, giving food in front of you while walking backwards away from the food on the floor.

- Repeat this process.

- Always reward away from the food on the floor by moving backwards when rewarding. This will encourage your dog to move away from the food and minimise the risk of your dog taking food from you and quickly eating the food off the floor.

- Walking backward will automatically turn the pressure on your dog's collar, so as soon as they feel the backward leash pressure, your dog will begin to learn to move with the leash and look at you.

- Ensure you say, 'LEAVE IT' before applying any pressure to your dog's collar.

- Making a 'reward event' such as a luring game feeding multiple rewards along with play and animation from you will help make you more valuable than items on the floor, along with giving your dog an extra positive experience.

This exercise will make leaving food/items on the floor to engage with you worth it.

Teaching LEAVE IT

https://me-qr.com/jUqi4iu7

Training 'LEAVE IT'

- As you approach the food on the floor, say, 'LEAVE IT', and if your dog leaves the food and looks at you, you should jackpot the behaviour without using leash pressure.

- Commence intermittent reinforcement by randomly rewarding the best efforts from your dog.

- Start adding a variety of food and items your dog likes to pick up off the floor.

- Try this training in new environments. Start in the

front yard and progress to the footpath, park, etc.

- Now that your dog understands what LEAVE IT means (i.e., your dog is looking at you in response to the command and not the leash pressure), you can use leash correction if your dog ignores the command. As your dog approaches the food, you command 'LEAVE IT', and if your dog continues towards the food or item, give a sharp pop on the lead and continue walking past.

- Punishment for not complying is vital for the longevity and reliability of this command, as the item on the floor may be of higher value than what you have to offer. A leash correction should be firm enough that your dog does not see the value in pursuing items on the floor, even if they are of high value.

- Drive to a new environment, leave your dog in the car and place food along the path where you will remember where it is. Walk past it. If your dog willingly leaves it, celebrate it, jackpot and keep moving on.

- Generalising this command is most necessary. If not, your dog will only perform the behaviour in comfortable and known environments.

Proofing 'LEAVE IT'

- In a new environment, when your dog willingly leaves food items alone and chooses not to sniff, praise and continue walking.

- If your dog chooses to approach it after saying 'LEAVE IT', issue a leash correction for non-compliance.

- Repeat above and intermittently & variably offer rewards.. Do this daily (at home, on walks, in the park, etc).

- A proofed level for this command will also mean your dog does not eat, scavenge, or pick up certain items off the floor as a result of the training process. The LEAVE IT command will be a way to communicate to your dog that you don't want them to engage with certain things.

- If you are walking off-leash and encounter prey (rabbit, cats, or birds), you should be able to say 'LEAVE IT', and your dog should continue walking along.

Drop an item

The DROP command tells the dog to let go of any object in its mouth, whether it is its toy or an item we want them to drop or let go of, such as a ball, tug, or even a sock!

There are many variations to this technique, and it can be challenging to cover all of them, as it starts to get more complex when we are teaching a dog to DROP a high-value item such as a tug, which is used as a reward. Incorrectly putting too much pressure may affect your game and relationship with your dog. Teaching this technique, like most others via words, brings a limitation that makes it difficult to explain all the steps in a way in which you can practice pragmatically. An in-person dog trainer can teach this with greater effectiveness.

Teaching 'DROP':

- Remember, if you have a hold of the item you wish your dog to let go of, the more you pull on it, the more your dog will pull back (opposition reflex). It would be best if you had a firm grip on the item but held it without any resistance for your dog to pull back on.

- The more you try to pull it out of your dog's mouth, the more your dog wants to keep it. Just like moving and struggling prey will cause a predator to be more active in killing it—once the prey dies and stops moving, the predator does not need to continue fighting the prey.

- Your dog's food or prey drive will determine what technique will work best for you.

- If your dog desires the item more than food, then it is unlikely your dog will want to let go of the item. If your dog has more food drive than the item you have, then your dog will not care to hold the item when food is present.

- The most effective way of teaching the DROP is by holding the item with a firm grip and relaxed arms and waiting your dog out.

- As your dog gets bored of this part of the game (it may take minutes, so take a seat), your dog will let go, and at that very moment, you MARK (with the marker for the tug) and play the game of tug immediately.

- Over time, with patience, your dog will associate relaxing your arms with letting go of the item. Then you can introduce the word 'DROP'), which gives your dog access to the game of tug or to fetch the ball.

- When your dog has a toy or ball in its mouth, hold the item with a firm grip yet relaxed arms, and present food in a closed fist in front of your dog's nose. The second your dog lets go of the item while trying to get the food in your hand, MARK 'YES' + REWARD.

- If you are using a ball or tug, reward with the ball or tug after you feed your dog.

- Continue playing this game whether you throw the item or play tug and repeat above.

- Once your dog reliably lets go of the item in your hand when they see your closed fist in front of their nose, you can start to introduce the verbal DROP command. Make sure you say drop BEFORE offering the closed fist.

- Intermittently jackpot the best efforts. Your dog sees the item you have as highly reinforcing, which may make it difficult to use the food to encourage your dog to let go.

- In this case, consider the following variation of this technique:

Teaching to DROP the tug

https://me-qr.com/H9k3IQVH

Teaching to DROP the ball

https://me-qr.com/zjDu8MaD

Training 'DROP'

- When training the DROP command, it is usually in the game of tug or throwing the ball, so with this in mind, it is essential to remember that the tug is the reward, and letting go of the tug is the behaviour you want your dog to do. Rewarding with the tug is the most effective way to play this game. If you have had success with relaxing the arms for your dog to let go, you should be able to play tug, and as soon as you say 'DROP' (relax and stay still), your dog should let go. Give your dog a few commands in a row before rewarding with the tug and continue to play the game.

Let your dog win the tug from time to time but be consistent with the DROP command.

- If you used the food technique, your dog should understand the word DROP, and a closed fist in front of their head means to drop the item. While your dog has the item in their mouth, say 'DROP' with a closed fist in front of their head (WITHOUT FOOD IN HAND). As soon as your dog drops the item, either reward with food or reward by throwing/playing tug with the item. We want your dog to understand that dropping the item is a part of the game and is what is necessary to continue playing. After ten successful repetitions of this stage of the DROP command, start implementing a pause between your dog dropping the item on command (a few seconds) before rewarding.

- If you are struggling and your dog will not drop the item and has shown that they are aware of the DROP command, you can follow the following step: While your dog is on a training collar and lead attached, you will give the verbal command 'DROP'. If your dog ignores the command, apply firm pressure (2/10) on the collar by the lead and hold the pressure until your dog drops the item, followed by 'YES' + REWARD.

- DO NOT CHOKE YOUR DOG. APPLY JUST ENOUGH PRESSURE ON THE COLLAR FOR IT TO BE UNCOMFORTABLE, BUT NOT TOO LITTLE PRESSURE, OR YOUR DOG WILL GET DESENSITISED TO LEASH PRESSURE.

- This training should generalise to other items away

from the ball and tug, e.g. a shoe, sock or a stick. Do this by having a leash on and food in the general vicinity so you can reinforce the behaviour effectively.

- If you have an issue with your dog picking up things they shouldn't, it is best to focus on teaching them to 'LEAVE IT' and good management so you don't set your dog up for failure (e.g., having them off the lead in the park or around things they usually pick up.)

Proofing 'DROP'

- Have your dog on a long lead with a medium-high distraction level present. Practice the DROP command. Ideally, in this stage, we are rewarding for the item they have dropped, whether it is a ball or a tug. Practice the DROP command at different distances, so your dog doesn't only drop items at your feet. Once you see your dog dropping an item at different distances from you, it reflects your dog's understanding of the command: drop the item (not bring it to me).

- By now, you should only be using your verbal 'DROP' for your dog to let go, no hand gesture or leash pressure, and it should be a commonly understood command. If your dog picks up a child's toy, you say 'DROP', and if your dog drops it immediately, praise it.

- Use the DROP in a chain of other behaviours—e.g.,

your dog brings the ball, you say,'DROP' then pick up the ball and issue other commands (DOWN, RECALL, MIDDLE), then reward your dog.

MIDDLE

The 'MIDDLE' command is to get your dog to position between your legs facing the same direction as you. It can be a great way to position your dog to minimise the space you and your dog take up.

For example, in a lift, your dog between your legs saves space for others, or in a busy line at the local markets.

It is also an effective command for dogs feeling intimidated or scared to find a position that makes them feel secure and safe. Or simply a cool party trick and part of your dog's training routine, as adding new commands to your repertoire prevents you and your dog from getting bored of the same basic commands.

MIDDLE is a positional command, meaning your dog must remain between your legs, facing the same direction as you, while walking and turning until your dog is released or rewarded with a ball or tug.

Teaching 'MIDDLE':

- Have your dog facing you. Start by having food in both hands and your dog off-leash in a secure area.

- You will lure your dog around the outside of your right leg and between your legs, facing the same direction as you, resulting in your dog's shoulders touching your inner thigh and your dog's head under your groin area.

- To begin, while your dog is facing you, lure your dog with your right hand to behind your right leg (luring around the outside of your leg to behind your knee), MARK + REWARD, and repeat this a few times.

- The next step is to have food in both hands. Lure with your right hand to the outside of your right leg and continue to lure with your left hand so that you can position your dog's head between your legs (the tricky part).

- Your left hand comes from under your groin so that you can lure your dog between your legs. You and your dog may get confused and frustrated, but stay persistent, reward any good effort, and keep sessions short.

- Reward once your dog moves from the front position to behind your right leg (right-hand lure) and transition to the left hand by meeting both the right and left hand together (between your legs).

- Your right-hand lures your dog from the right-hand side of your right leg, and your left hand lures between your legs into the finished position.

- Have plenty of food in your left hand to reward multiple times while luring your dog from behind to between your legs. It may make it easier to take a small step forward to help position your dog.

- Doing this on the spot without your feet moving may make it difficult, depending on the size of your dog, so take a few small steps forward to align your dog to come between your legs.

- Once your dog can be lured into the MIDDLE with food between your legs 10 out of 10 times, start introducing the verbal command 'MIDDLE'.

- Remember to issue your verbal commands one second before you lure him.

- Introduce the 'OK' release command to tell your dog when to get out of position.

- Start weaning off having food in your right hand and only having food in your left hand once you have implemented the verbal command.

- Jackpot when your dog performs behaviour with more enthusiasm and clarity.

Teaching MIDDLE

https://me-qr.com/hUvd1VTh

Training 'MIDDLE':

- In this phase, you should start weaning off food in your hands using your hands as non-verbal cues and rewarding your dog as soon as they enter the middle position as you like.

- Randomly reward when your dog comes into the middle position and gives you focused eye contact.jackpot the good efforts. Make sure your requirements are that your dog is between your legs, shoulders touching your inner thigh, and your dog's head is looking up, giving you eye contact. This is important as you do not want your dog to be too far ahead of you where they cannot see or feel you.

- Eye contact and shoulders touching your inner thighs (or shins for smaller dogs) are essential for the proceeding steps. The physical touch and eye contact allow your dog to stick between you while walking forwards, backward, and directional changes. Otherwise, you may have to help your dog more when adding the movement piece to this command.

- Once your dog starts coming into position and looking at you, ready for the reward, begin to add directional changes. Start with a 90° right turn using your right hand to turn right. Keep your lure hand close to your legs when doing the 90° turn, and ensure your feet move with your lure to position your dog correctly. Do the same thing for the left 90° turn, use your left hand when turning left.

- Once your dog can make positional changes, start to implement forward stepping. Start by rewarding the first two steps and increase accordingly.

- Teaching directional changes before adding forward steps is preferred to help your dog stay between your legs and use the lure and feel of your movement. If you start walking forward before training directionals, your dog may tend to speed ahead and break position. Remember to reward intermittently in this phase of the training.

- Your dog can now come into the MIDDLE and start taking some steps in the same direction and do 90° turns. You can now offer a SIT or DOWN command in the middle position. Reward and release out of position.

- Once you have taught the behaviour with food and have a reliable position from your dog, you can start to reward with a ball, tug, or jackpot if your dog can hold the middle while taking ten steps, adding left and right turns, and following extra commands.

- Once your dog can successfully enter the middle position on command with no food, walk in the same direction while in MIDDLE and will perform other commands such as SIT and DOWN until being released. It is time to start adding more distractions and performing this command in a more active environment, starting with your front yard.

Proofing 'MIDDLE':

- From a down-stay, give the MIDDLE command for your dog to come into position, give the DOWN command again, walk away (while your dog stays down) and release your dog.

- While walking, say 'MIDDLE' and walk in different directions, stop intermittently and continue walking again. Issue 'DOWN' while your dog is walking between your legs. Switch up the location, duration and distance of the MIDDLE as you continue your practice.

- Start thinking about how this can be used in practical situations, either keeping your dog safe from other dogs or people in public spaces(e.g., having lunch at the coffee shop or being used as part of training exercises for extra mental stimulation).

- While your dog is off the lead and doing their own thing, give the MIDDLE command and walk, keeping your dog in the MIDDLE before returning to doing their own thing. Working with this command often will ensure you proof the command to have an actual function and to be reliable behaviour on cue.

HEEL position

- The primary function of teaching the HEEL command is to have a command for your dog to stand and walk on the left-hand side of your body while staring at your face. A verbal command to tell your dog to position next to you without using a lure, gesture or leash pressure.

- It is useful when you want your dog to your left-hand side at any time and while in a DOWN, MIDDLE or 'BED' command. If not taught, then it can be clunky and confusing for your dog when you want them to be next to you without training this behaviour on cue.

- Teaching dogs to heel is a popular and very competitive thing in the dog training world. It is also a piece of traditional advice when walking a do..For example, you must always say 'HEEL' when you start walking your dog. What we will learn in this training book is that HEEL is a focused position, not a way to walk loose lead in general. Your dog should always walk with a loose lead by your side without a verbal command.

- In competitive sport dog training, the 'focused heel' is a behaviour taught to a dog to stay 100% laser-focused on the handler (intense stare) while walking around the field with high drive, enthusiasm, and commitment. This type of training is fascinating and complex and worth teaching your dog. However, in the scope of this book, you will be introduced to the HEEL command merely as a positional command for your dog to come to your left-hand side. This can be the foundation on which you take your HEELING journey to the next level. Because of this, I will only provide this command's teaching and training phase.

Teaching 'HEEL':

- While your dog is facing you, lure with your right hand to your left knee while simultaneously taking a step back with your left leg. MARK + REWARD when your dog's nose is lured to your left knee. Immediately after rewarding, step your left leg back to a natural standing position and again MARK + REWARD.

- Because the HEEL is a positional command, it is an excellent habit to start from the beginning to release your dog ('OK') after rewarding and reward after releasing to ensure your dog knows that they need to hold this new behaviour for a set amount of duration before being released out of the HEEL.

- Performing the action of luring your dog, stepping back and forth again, will allow your dog to move their body from facing you to turning along to your left-hand side and facing the same direction as you are while having your dog's head aligned with your hip.

- Remember, wherever your lure hand goes (your dog's head), your dog's rear end will face the opposite direction. Luring in motion while you move your left leg back and forth will help your dog swing their rear end around so that their front legs pivot when taking that step forward into a natural stance.

- Do not reward your dog for sitting while being next to you. You want to keep your dog standing while teaching and training the HEEL position. Of course, later in training, we will issue SIT & DOWN when in the HEEL; however, you want to ensure your dog is standing at your left-hand side. A common mistake is before rewarding; you may lift your hand slightly while luring your dog into position, raising your luring hand is a cue to SIT. Remember to MARK + REWARD while dog is standing along side you and keep your hand still to ensure your dog understands the position you want them to be in.

- Some dogs need extra assistance when luring into the HEEL as they may lose interest or get confused. Movement motivates dogs, so, taking a few steps back when luring to your left knee may help encourage your dog to come alongside you before stepping forward to align them into the HEEL position. Rewarding multiple times during the luring process (having plenty of food in your hand) is also necessary to keep your dog committed to the activity.

- Once your dog comes into the HEEL position 10/10 times with your feet moving back and forth, it is time to lure your dog into the HEEL position by only luring your hands. This is where we can transition the lure hand from the right to the left hand. Use your left hand to lure into the HEEL position. MARK + REWARD when your dog's head aligns with your left hip.

- Only name the behaviour 'HEEL' if your dog comes into the HEEL position 10/10 times in a row, the way you like it to look. Don't name it until you love it. Remember to say 'HEEL' one second before luring into position (word before lure).

- Using leash pressure in the learning phase can help prime your dog in the training phase to ensure your dog is in the correct position without relying only on your food lure. To introduce leash pressure, say the word 'HEEL', and with your left hand, use a 1/10 pressure on the lead along with the food lure in your right hand. Leash pressure moves in the direction of your luring. Release pressure immediately when your dog is in the correct position simultaneously MARK + REWARD.

Training 'HEEL':

- When in the training phase, you need to start rewarding intermittently for your dog coming into the HEEL, and your dog should be comfortable with leash pressure to help guide them into the HEEL.

- The HEEL command is a positional behaviour, so teaching your dog to stick by your side when turning on the spot (left or right about turns) before progressing to walking forward is better. The HEEL looks like a forward-moving command, but if you can teach your dog to stay next to you while performing the behaviour, what you want becomes apparent to your dog in the long term.

- If you teach walking forward first before teaching to turn, you may find your dog getting confused when you start to spin after moving forward. This can make your dog break position, do wide births away from you or jump up with excitement now that you have introduced something new.

- While your dog is in HEEL, start by doing a 90° turn to your left-hand side, MARK + REWARD if your dog stays in position while having to move their back legs around with you. Release, 'OK', and repeat. Finish on a positive note.

- Using some leash pressure to help guide your dog can help, only use soft guiding pressure, and always release when your dog is in the desired position. Taking your time with this is essential.

- Practice your 90° right turns, ensuring your dog stays tight next to your left hip when following your food lure.

- Switch between right and left turns before releasing. Remember to jackpot the best behaviours, intermittently make a fun game (reward event) when making it more challenging and always finish positively.

- Reward one step at a time when introducing forward walking in the HEEL. You do not want to start walking too much forward too quickly, as your dog may break too often. It can be exciting for you to start this next step, so be mindful to go slow.

- You should be able to say 'HEEL' and use your hand gesture (no food in hand) into position one second later. Make sure you MARK the behaviour you like BEFORE your hand goes to the pouch to issue a reward.

- Start using a ball/tug to reward your dog for HEELING if your dog is motivated by this type of reinforcement.

- HEEL position for four steps forward, left turn for four steps and right turn before releasing should be a reasonable requirement before practising HEEL in a more distracting environment.

- Start in the driveway before practising on walks and around other stimuli.

- While on a walk, stop, DOWN your dog, walk away, and say HEEL. When your dog comes into position, MARK + REWARD. If you need to use a small amount of leash pressure into position, as long as your dog looks at you, MARK + REWARD intermittently.

- When you do not reward, give another command (SIT or DOWN) before releasing (OK). Vary in which sequence you give your commands, e.g., 'HEEL' to 'DOWN', walk away 'COME'. Don't be too predictable.

Benefits of trick training

There are a myriad of tricks and complex skills you can teach your dog that are fun, engaging and a stimulating activity for both you and your dog.

You can easily add extracurricular activities to your training routine with the fundamentals explained here. I recommend teaching the basics first as they have more function and are foundational to the intermediate and advanced training.

Dogs with higher drive and energy (working type breeds, but not limited to) benefit the most from trick training as they need the extra stimulation. Also, introducing more tricks and complex skills becomes more fun as we can get bored of the same basic commands over time.

Dogs with play/prey drive that love to chase the ball and play tug usually need the most regular and consistent training as their high-drive nature demands a mental and physical outlet.

When training with the ball or tug, you want it to remain fun and exciting, so it is recommended to teach new commands and advance the skill set your dog has.

After months of this training/exercise routine, you will find it refreshing to teach and train new behaviours to keep the flare of training along with the engagement you will experience from your dog.

Extra training, such as agility, flyball, scent sports, protection sports, herding, etc., are the next level up from basic obedience and tricks. You would usually join a club/community focusing on a particular style and training more specific to your dogs breed, age, energy level, drive and of course your interests.

I highly recommended extra training for those dogs that were bred to work. This helps facilitate optimal fulfillment, which creates a calm and balanced dog.

My dog Chilli

https://me-qr.com/Z2v6aPvK

6
The Mindset of a Leader

Leadership

To be a leader, it's not enough to act like a leader; you must be a leader. Developing skills to be an effective leader is essential to have the best relationship, control, and communication with your dog. The leadership skills you learn while training your dog may also benefit you in general life.

A leader guides, disciplines, helps, and protects others. Leadership is not only about control and dominance; it must also include compassion, empathy, firmness, and fairness. Love does not always equate to respect in humans and dogs, but by learning the mindset of a leader you can create a relationship that your dog can rely on, and in turn, you can depend on them.

There are two common types of leadership—direct and authoritative or engaged & team player. The most efficient and effective leaders are well-versed in both types.

Being direct and authoritative is necessary for your role in the training process because you need to keep your dog safe, and well-mannered, and give them an understanding of their boundaries. In time this develops good habits and a healthy mindset for your dog who will view you as a strong leader to follow.

When using a direct leadership approach, assertiveness should not be confused with aggressiveness. To be assertive is to be calm, controlled, and firm. Aggression is a sign of frustration, fear, and lack of control. You should not scare your dog into submission. You want to direct and guide via assertive techniques and qualities that create submission by respecting boundaries rather than through fear. Your dog should not be terrified to express itself.

The other form of leadership is engaging and guiding through play and encouragement, similar to how a team player sport is conducted. To lead with cooperation with each other through games, play, and engagement.

Cooperation is not simply following rules but by both handler and dog focused on the same task to work within the constraints to achieve the reward/goal. This animated way of expressing oneself requires your dog to be willing to participate and earn rewards and affection from you. Typically, when playing games of tug, for example, it is about working together, learning that the commands and behaviours being told are the way to play the game.

Choosing one leadership style can limit your effectiveness in training but combining the two will allow you to tap into both forms of motivation, depending on the situation at hand. Dogs in different situations will be motivated by either external stimuli or you, and diverse expressions of leadership will be required in each scenario.

Suppose your dog feels more motivated to chase the rabbit

than to engage with you and your potential reward (play, tug, food, and affection). In that case, you will need to be assertive and provide a consequence to communicate to your dog to stop chasing the rabbit immediately. Sometimes your dog may see the rabbit in the distance and has a low drive to pursue it but is willing to follow and play with you, so this style of leadership is more appropriate. Good leaders set their followers up for success, and management must always be exercised.

A human example for both forms of leadership: The direct and authoritative form of leadership (masculine form) can be seen in the military when a superior issues a command to their inferior in a state of urgency during training. It is a 'following the rules or face the consequences' kind of command.

On the other side (feminine form) is the more engaging = and playful leadership style like you see in a waltz or salsa dance. One leads, and the other follows. This type is not forced. It is in the love of the dance and cannot exist with two leaders or two followers. Otherwise, the beauty of the dance will not exist.

To be clear, masculine does not mean male, and feminine does not mean female; this is not gender specific. In my belief, to be an effective and efficient leader, one must embrace both qualities and integrate them into one's personality and character.

A great leader will lead with compassion and love but will not budge on the firm rules that have been set, knowing that discipline equals freedom. It is your primary job to provide, protect, and love your dog.

Being a responsible owner

You must take complete ownership and exercise total responsibility as a dog owner, as our dogs are not fit to make civilized decisions based on societal expectations. You are responsible for your dog's actions legally, socially, and familially. Learning ways to communicate, control, and integrate your training into your daily activities should be considered to be the best dog owner you can be.

By law, you are responsible for your dog and what they choose to do, and it begins with appropriate management systems in place. You are the one that gives your dog access to the world and the environments they engage with. If you fail to plan, you plan to fail, so make sure you are using the appropriate equipment—housing, collars, leads, and nutrition. Take measures to ensure your dog cannot escape your yard; purchase a solid and useful crate; invest in the best collars and leads you can afford that have been pressure tested, and research the best food for your dog to maintain a healthy body and mind.

Effective management also includes following the laws and rules of your council/state and keeping your dog under control at all times. If you do not manage your dog appropriately, they will learn disobedience, which makes training more difficult. Mismanaging dogs does not set them up for success, and it will be hard for them to learn what you want to teach them.

If your dog does not have a solid recall, it is irresponsible to let them off the lead and expect, by luck, that they will come when you call. To be responsible would be to attach a long lead and practice recall in your dog's free time. Owning your responsibility means you must be able to respond, and this means you should know your dog well enough to learn and actively apply management strategies and training protocols to your daily life.

Understanding your dog's biology and psychology will help you determine what will fulfill them and allow them to be the best version of themselves. Learn and study what dogs need in general and, more specifically, what the breed needs based on the function they served in their traditional roles (what they were initially bred for). This will allow you to implement techniques in daily life that will help your dog to be content and well-adjusted to domestic living, which usually doesn't just happen on its own.

Being active and not lazy is a fundamental requirement of being a responsible dog owner, as your habits become your dog's habits. If you do not facilitate a way of life that your dog can function appropriately in this world, it will be difficult for your dog to learn skills, develop good manners, and be content. It's a good practice to be proactive, not reactive.

Making excuses will not help you or your dog. We can all find a reason to explain why we don't do things we ought to, but this won't help you or your dog in the long run. Allow your journey with your dog to compel you to commit fully to your obligations, at least for your dog's sake. If dogs can teach us one thing, it is to be the best version of ourselves for them. Making excuses for not regularly walking, training, feeding, and playing with your dog, reflects poorly on you as the owner because your dog depends on you completely for guidance. Being consistent and competent is key to gaining positive results and respect over time. Being a leader is about accepting responsibility for all potential outcomes.

Thinking 15 steps ahead

The mindset of a leader is to guide their followers in a forward direction toward an ultimate goal. Just like the grandmaster chess player, each move is set up for the next 15 moves to follow, and like a builder laying a solid foundation, preparing for a big and tall dwelling to build on top of is critical.

To be the most effective in your dog training journey, you must understand that the techniques you use at each stage are essential building blocks for your dog's future behaviours. Keeping this in mind will optimize each training session and help prepare for the next. It's important to always keep the bigger picture in mind.

Planning 15 steps ahead means you must be clear on your goals and stick to your plan by being consistent. To be effective with your training and behaviour modification, you must set up each session to address both strengths and weaknesses of you and your dog so that you aim at finishing each session on a positive note, moving closer to your goals. If you and your dog fail in any way, you must treat it as a learning lesson and recover from it to allow improvement and growth to come from the experience.

Leaders think and operate for the bigger picture and understand that good things take time and include practice, patience, and persistence. Focusing 15 steps ahead allows you to be focused on what is important, mastering every step along the way and developing delayed gratification. This helps you focus on your mission and goals so you don't give up. 'When the going gets tough, the tough get going' is a saying that comes to mind as obstacles and curve balls come your way. Don't allow challenges to be the catalyst to giving up, instead, do the opposite—push forward and stay consistent with your plan.

If you only plan 3-5 steps ahead, you may achieve your goals, which on the surface looks great; however, this may tempt you to slow down in your daily training and you may settle for less than you can achieve. Even worse, old and undesirable behaviour from your dog may return.

Your dog relies on you for daily structure, which means it must be purposeful, and you should be aiming at the slightly unachievable goals. This keeps you driven and motivated to maintain a healthy and consistent approach to your training.

An example would be a goal to have your dog down-stay off-leash in front of a coffee shop for 10 minutes in a highly distracting environment while you are out of sight. For some dogs, this seems unattainable but is a great goal to have as it compels you to train your dog with purpose, even though it may seem impossible.

Consistently work on developing your skills to allow your dog more experience and freedom. Training your dog to function in day-to-day life is the best place to start. A leader leads with compassion and firmness toward a particular goal, so set your goals further than you think you can reach and break each stage down to an achievable standard.

Thinking 15 steps ahead is a professional's mindset in any field and area of expertise and is an excellent skill to adopt in your dog training. Continually reassess your goals and maintain effectiveness in your skills, communication, and relationship with your dog. You must be the best leader possible by always aiming high and taking care of your responsibilities daily.

Situational awareness

Knowing what's going on around you at all times is indeed a life skill that everyone should develop, especially when training your dog. This essential survival mindset is particularly important when walking a fearful, reactive, aggressive dog and young puppies. Developing the skill of being aware of your dog's specific triggers (other dogs, people, trucks) can help you be more proactive with the handling and training application.

If you are walking down the street and spot a dog 100 m away, and you know your dog will start barking and lunging when the dog is 50 m away, you have the opportunity to execute the proper training technique before an incident occurs. Being aware of the dog in the distance also allows you to cross the road, make some space, or change direction if you think that's the appropriate decision.

The problem with not having situational awareness is that your dog will react to the trigger before you know what is happening; this leads to your dog's behaviour being reinforced or, even worse, your dog attacking, causing injury and the drama associated. You want your dog to trust you, for you to have their back. You can only take control of a situation if you are aware of it.

Additional things to try when walking with your dog besides being equipped with the right equipment, food, etc., are:

- Keeping your head up, and scan your environment from time to time in a calm and controlled way- not paranoid and tense;

- Keeping your phone in your pocket, and if you have music playing or you are listening to Life With Your Dog Podcast, keep only one headphone in at a low level to make sure you can hear what's happening around you;

- Being aware of your dog's body language and any subtle or apparent changes. Scan the environment, and get your dog's focus on you;

- Being proactive and less reactive. Making decisions and applying techniques while your dog is not overly aroused, rather than after something happens and trying to make behaviour changes in times of stress.

- Applying this practice daily. Understand what is occurring around you; it may save your life one day.

7

The Structured Walk

Leash locking

When handling your lead, you must make sure you have it secure in your hand for many reasons. Safety is the number one reason why learning leash locking is very important, especially with larger, powerful dogs.

I also leash lock with smaller dogs for comfort and developing good habits.

Don't wrap the lead around your hand in a bundle)

Try the following:

1. Hold lead in left hand, palm facing down, knuckles facing up (how you would hold a bike handle).
2. Fold the handle side of the lead over your thumb.
3. Grip the lead by fingers clamping the lead into your palm.
4. Keep your thumb parallel to your fingers.
5. Check video on QR or link below.

Leash locking prevents the lead from slipping out of your

hand when your dog lunges forward or pulls back on the lead.

It also helps with handling when walking and training by giving you a firm grip while still being able to relax your elbow and shoulder.

Holding a lead firmly in your hand but relaxed in the rest of your arm allows you to have good control if your dog is to run ahead, but when your dog is next to you, there is no tension in the lead.

Your dog needs to know the difference in leash pressure and cannot always have pressure on the lead when walking or training. This works regardless of individual strength, the technique of leash looping over the thumb creates the lock and anchor in your hand.

Holding the lead bundled in your hand or wrapped tight makes you tense your fingers to hold tight, which tightens up your whole arm.

If you hold the lead tight, your dog will be uncomfortable, confused, and tense. You will suffer a sore and potentially injured arm from handling your dog on the lead.

Make leash locking the way you always hold the lead for comfort, safety, and effectiveness. Most of all, develop good habits so your dog does not run free when you least expect it.

If your arm is relaxed but ready to apply pressure or correction, it will improve your overall timing and effectiveness.

Leash locking

https://me-qr.com/lnc7GFXG

The walk 20/20/20 rule

Walking your dog should be a daily routine. It is an essential activity for many reasons and is one of the most critical tools and jobs to give your domestic dog. Since most domestic dogs do not have a traditional job, we must facilitate a daily ritual, routine, and activity. Walking is a way to free your dog from boredom, release pent-up physical energy, and provide them with mental stimulation (mind-body connection) and the opportunity to continue seeing the world around them. We must remember that the walk is also for our own physical and mental well-being, which is another critical reason why a stress-free loose leash walk is essential.

How you will learn to walk your dog will become a dynamic experience for you and your dog. Since it is a daily ritual, we want it to be free of stress on both sides of the lead. Your dog's goal is to walk on a loose lead next to you. When you stop, they stop. If you say sit, they sit and once you say 'OK', your dog walks loose lead next to you.

The more you practice teaching your dog to walk by your side, the better leader you become and a better follower your dog becomes. Your walk is not only a physical exercise, it should also be mental, by teaching your dog to follow the rules (thinking) while still walking (moving). When this mind-body connection is in play, you will experience a calm, relaxing walk rather than a chaotic whirlwind. We want a fulfilled dog, not just a tired one.

You will learn that every walk will have three parts (the 20/20/20 rule), assuming you are going on a 60 minute walk—20 minute structured loose lead walk to a park, 20 minutes of long lead time in the park, and a 20 minute loose lead walk back home. This walking routine is for every day. You want to allow your dog to learn that the short lead while walking the streets is a job, to be focused and follow you. The walk should also be fun and appropriate which means giving your dog time to pee, poop, play, have training sessions for the ball, and have free time to do as they please. This is what the free time on a 10 m lead facilitates for your dog. Once that time is up, take a 20-minute walk back home in a structured and relaxed manner.

Loose lead walking

- The walk starts when you attach a lead to the collar. Ensure all collars are fitted appropriately right from the beginning of the walk (inside your property). Keeping collar high on neck, behind the ears and under the jaw for effective control and not applying excessive pressure through the leash.

- Always leash lock while holding the lead. Make it a habit!

- Be calm, and do not overexcite your dog when in this process.

- A good habit is to practice a training session while on the lead before leaving the house. This will help your dog regulate their excitement levels and allow you to achieve focus and attentiveness from your dog. Attaching your lead and collar for every training session (when not going for a walk) will desensitise your dog to the lead (it does not become a promise that you are going for a walk).

- When approaching the door/gate, tell your dog to sit and wait for the door to be opened before releasing ('OK') to walk through the door. Ensure you are between your dog and the door when they are in a SIT so that your dog can see you and knows not to pass you when the door opens. Don't have your dog between you and the door. Otherwise, your dog will rush out the doorway, pulling you over and creating bad habits.

- Ensure you walk through the door first for safety reasons and create order around this part of the routine.

- If your dog jumps and runs through the door, change direction, walk back through the doorway, and start over until your dog is calm walking through the doorway. If this takes 5 minutes, then so be it, this is part of the walk and should be taken out of the allocated walking time.

- When on the walk, reward with high-value food every time your dog is next to you (eyes in line with your knee) and ensure it is a loose lead.

Once your dog gets in front of you (don't wait for tension on the lead), you can practice what has been shown throughout your training session to correct their behaviour.

Here are three ways to correct your dog from getting ahead of you and pulling against the leash. **Ensure your dog's collar remains high on neck, behind the ears and under the jaw**:

- **Change direction by turning left or right**. The right about turn will activate leash pressure for your dog to adhere to. Once your dog catches up with you, leash pressure turns off naturally. The left about turn utilises spacial pressure of your body abruptly turns and faces your dog as you continue to walk in the opposite direction. Once your dog adheres and re-positions on your left-hand side, your dog will feel comfortable again. Changing direction randomly will encourage your dog to check in on you regularly.

- **Leash pressure.** Using leash pressure is the default technique that gets used most on your walks. Upward pressure is applied to the slip lead or collar when your dog starts to get ahead of you and released when your dog positions next to you. Don't wait for a leash to go tight. As soon as your dog's head gets ahead of your left knee, turn on the pressure (2/10 consistent pressure) and immediately remove it once the dog is in the correct position next to you on your left-hand side.

- **Leash pop.** This leash correction is a short-sharp pop (across your body from left to right) that is a punishment for behaviour—used if leash pressure has been used three times in five seconds or for the behaviour you never want to be displayed (jumping, peeing in an unacceptable spot, jumping on someone, barking, etc.).

To correct, either change your direction; apply pressure to the collar upwards (90°up to the sky), and as soon as your dog comes back next to you, release pressure and reward ('YES' + REWARD). *The pressure release technique is the default technique while walking.*

Finally, you can pop the lead (always pull the lead across your body to put pressure on the side of your dog's neck. DO NOT pull back where you can put tension on the trachea.)

The goal is that you want your dog to remain by your side while walking. Your dog's peripheral vision is on you (not staring at you) while keeping a loose lead.

You want to teach your dog to walk next to you, not focusing on stopping them from pulling. This is an important distinction as you want to focus on what you want your dog to do and not put all your focus on what you do not want them to do.

If your dog is next to you, they can see you; if your dog can see you, they can focus on you; if your dog can focus on you, there is more of a chance that they will listen to you. This is why we prioritise keeping our dogs in line with us so that they keep us in their peripheral vision while they enjoy the walk too. When you approach the road, always get your dog to sit until being released with an 'OK'.

It is always a good idea to practice your training commands while on the walk (SIT, DOWN, STAY, COME, LOOK, etc.). This will help encourage your dog to bond and focus on you and keep them interested in you.

Also, the more you practice your training outside of the house in new and exciting environments, the stronger these commands become, which will help when you need them in real-life applications. (DOWN-STAY at the coffee shop; COME when called if they run out the front door; focus on you when there are many people and dogs around).

Practice when you do not need it so you have it ready to go when you do need it.

Reward as much as possible in the early days during your loose lead walking when your dog is next to you to reinforce their behaviour. You aim to show your dog where you want them to walk—next to you with a loose leash.

While walking, it is good to say your dog's name, and as soon as they look at you, 'YES' + REWARD. This is essential. You need their focus and engagement on you before giving commands, especially in busy environments.

As soon as you are about to correct your dog (1 second before), make sure you give a verbal correction ('UH-UH'). This is because you want to give your dog the opportunity to come back next to you without having to use a physical correction. If you must correct your dog, use the least amount of pressure possible.

Your correction is supposed to be an uncomfortable sensation to weaken the behaviour for the future—not to be used to inflict pain or fear. If you cannot do this correctly or have yet to be shown how, only practise leash corrections once a professional has shown you how to execute them appropriately.

There is no verbal command for loose lead walking. The short lead attached to the collar means stay to my left-hand side unless given commands or directions. When the lead is attached, it is your responsibility to be consistent and clear with your dog about what is expected.

A great way to practice keeping your dog's focus on you during walks is to randomly change the speed, stopping intermittently, and then continue walking. This unpredictability will help your dog stay focused and at your pace. Otherwise, your dog will walk the general momentum of how you usually walk and in autopilot (not paying attention to you).

Making time to practice tethering/tie-out exercises is great practice for the future. If you can, build up to 5 minutes of your dog being tied to a pole or post (ensuring it's secure) while you intermittently go out of sight (preferably in a down-stay).

You want this to be a regular part of the walk so when you want to go into the coffee shop quickly, help someone with something, or play with the kids at the playground, your dog will know how to behave on their own.

Without this training, your dog will be stressed or anxious which causes barking, chewing the leash, and freaking out.

Loose leash walking tips

https://me-qr.com/TvE6PJhM

Loose leash walking techniques

https://me-qr.com/iDFT9qtp

Long lead-free time

Once you arrive at the park, attach your 10 m lead to your dog's collar. It is helpful to have a verbal command for the long lead time. I say 'GO', but commands such as 'FREE' or 'BREAK' work well too. It does not matter which word you use as long as you're consistent. I prefer a verbal command for a long lead time to cue our dog that it's time to play and be free. I use the short lead on walks as the default behaviour.

Long lead-free time is a great time to practice your training (SIT, DOWN, RECALL, and other commands that are part of your training routine). If your dog is motivated by playing with a tug or ball, use this to reward commands, otherwise, use food treats.

The more you practice long lead time, the more you teach your dog to follow you and your commands while at a distance, building confidence and setting boundaries.

Be aware of how you hold the lead to reduce the likelihood of injury. If your dog is to run away toward another dog, person, or just zoomies, step on the lead to remove the pressure from your hands. Be sure to step on a leash with your heel and not the ball of your foot. Your heel has more body weight, whereas the ball/toes of your foot are not as secure, and the lead can slip through. Leash locking is always a recommended way of holding the lead to prevent rope burn or accidental release of the lead. Always wear enclosed shoes when operating a long lead (not flip-flops or barefoot), especially for larger breeds and while your dog is getting used to long lead etiquette.

If your dog is too powerful to have access to the entire 10 m of the leash, give only 3-5 m length by locking keeping the rest of the free line loose on the floor (don't bunch up the rest of the leash in your hands as it gets messy and unsafe to handle).

Free time is not entirely free, as your dog is not allowed to run away from you, especially if you do not have a reliable recall or down stay. But it is a time to have fun, run, and essentially be a dog while still knowing they must follow you for safety and develop good habits. Long lead time is a stepping stone to teaching your dog how to behave when off the lead (where your dog is allowed off lead in leash-free environments, on private property, or if your dog happens to slip out of your hands).

Long lead time is best done in the middle of the walk (20/20/20 rule) and should be done as a daily practice. A long lead time at the beginning of the walk-over excites your dog for the walk, and a long lead time at the end excites your dog when it is time to return home. Once the long lead-free time is over, attach a short lead to their collar and walk home in the structured manner described above.

8

House Manners: Master Your Castle

Toilet training

Teaching your dog to be toilet trained is essential, especially if you enjoy your dog sharing the home with you. For some dogs, toilet training seems to come naturally with minimal effort from their owners; however, for other dogs, it can feel like the hardest thing to teach them. Toilet training should begin when your dog is a puppy, but if you get an untrained dog when they are an adult, it can be more challenging. Other challenges include moving houses, looking after someone's dog, etc., when you may notice that the dog doesn't see an issue with eliminating wherever and whenever they wish.

Setting you and your dog up for success leads to a fully toilet-trained dog, along with consistency from the other members of your home. Most adult dogs that are healthy and relaxed should be able to hold their bladder and bowels for up to 8 hours, usually at night when everyone is asleep. Over time you will notice your dog won't accidentally toilet in your home unless taken to the allocated area, but this takes time and consistency.

Before starting your toilet training, you must be clear about where you want your dog to toilet and if they have adequate access to that area in a timeframe you know your dog can hold. You must also acknowledge that your management and training must be adjusted accordingly if your dog is overly stressed with anxiety, unwell with loose stools, urinary tract infections, or a senior dog.

The following advice is for dogs that do not know where you would like them to go to toilet. The goal will differ depending on your living setup, whether you live in a house, apartment, granny flat, etc. Because of this, the advice following will need to be applied to your specific circumstances.

The first thing to remember is that management is the most important thing when training most behaviours, especially toilet training! Please don't leave your dog unattended in a place where you do not want them to mess it up. If you are to leave the room, ensure they are in a secured place where they are allowed to eliminate, like the backyard or balcony or left in their crate. If you don't catch them in the act, all you can do is clean it up and move on, so set yourself and your dog up for success. Until your dog is fully toilet trained, keep a leash attached to collar while free in your home to easily get control of your dog and move him to the desired location. Keep the following in mind:

- Dogs usually eliminate (pee and poop) as soon as they wake up after eating and after exercise. Be observant and allow your dog to eliminate in the correct area immediately after these times of the day.

- When your dog is inside with you, make sure you take them to the desired place you like them to go toilet every 40-60 minutes, ideally on the grass in your backyard or outside. If you're in an apartment, it will be the pee pads/fake grass on the balcony, in the laundry room or ideally on grass out the front of the building complex.

- When your dog is peeing or pooping in the desired location, repeat the word 'TOILET', and when they finish, 'YES' and reward.

- If your dog goes in the wrong spot (and you catch them in the act), pick them up midway or take them by the lead and walk them/ take them to the desired location. DO NOT get crazy and scare your dog otherwise they will hide from you to do their business.

- Clean up areas with a mop and disinfectant, followed by a spray of white vinegar mixed with some water. Most of the smell in urine is due to ammonia, a highly alkaline substance. Vinegar is acidic and helps to neutralise this scent.

- If your dog is in the backyard and is toileting in an undesired location, such as pavers or the patio area, it's best to clean it up and feed them in the same place that you do not want them to eliminate. Dogs do not like to eat where they eliminate, scatter feeding (throwing food directly onto the ground) works best if possible.

- Cleaning poop daily is also essential, as dogs do not like to poop on top of existing poop and will start pooping in other areas of your space. If your dog poops on the pavers and the grass, clean up the whole yard and feed your dog on the pavers. This will eventually teach your dog that the paved area is a feeding area and that the grass is for the toilet. This rule applies to all areas of the house and apartments. If you regularly pick up poop, you may notice your dog pooping in the same place over time.

- For male dogs that mark in all areas of the yard, you can collect another male dog's urine by giving a friend an old towel to place on top of their male dog's urine. With the same towel, put it in an area of your yard you wish for your dog to pee on (usually the back of your yard). There are pheromone sticks that are supposed to achieve the same thing that you could try.

- Crate training is a highly recommended and an excellent option which is highly effective for toilet training and managing your dog for several reasons (refer to the Crate Training section).

Barking issues

Barking can be a big problem for dog owners, especially for the neighbours who have to deal with the annoyance. Most barking issues are attention-seeking behaviours. However, it can also be a fearful response to something happening in or around the house like the presence of prey. Your dog could also have separation distress or anxiety.

Finding out why your dog is barking is the first step before taking action to eliminate the problem behaviour. Observe and understand why your dog is barking by either watching through a window (be hidden, your dog is not supposed to know you are watching) or using a camera and watching from further away from where your dog is,either a baby monitor, video call or surveillance systems.

Most problematic behaviour is usually a symptom of a lack of structure, routine and stimulation in your dog's life. The steps below are techniques specific to barking. However, it is not the only remedy to eliminating this problem. Consider the whole picture of your dog's life and what entails a typical day. Fulfil their mind and body through the regular practice of obedience training, enrichment and exercise to get the best out of your dog so they are not looking for ways to find purpose in their day. Give your dog a job.

On the other hand, it could be a behaviour that you have developed by a lack of management and training while your dog was a pup or when you first acquired your dog. Routine and thinking ahead is a mindset that needs to be exercised because the habits you develop will become your dog's habits.

Dogs bark for different reasons:

- Barking at something
- Attention seeking
- Separation distress/anxiety
- Health issue/ injury

Barking at something

Some dogs are not barking to be let inside the house or for

you to join them in the yard, they are barking because they see something like a person or dog walking past your home, a possum or bird, children next door playing or other sounds that may either startle or excite them. Stopping all barking issues can be tricky, but this form of barking can be a little more challenging as you are not a part of the equation.

Remember, you only have 1.6 seconds to reward or correct your dog for barking when they see the stimulus. This makes catching the behaviour in the act difficult, so proper observation is the first step to eliminating the barking. Set your dog up for success by being clear that the barking is unacceptable, reinforcing the behaviour when it does not occur, and strengthening the behaviour you would like to repeat in the future.

Depending on the stimulus, your dog will either be in prey drive or defence drive when exposed. Prey drive is when your dog wants what they engage with, such as prey animals or fast-moving objects. Defence drive is when your dog wants something they engage with to go away, such as a person or dog walking past the fence line.

When your dog barks out of prey drive, it is because your dog lacks impulse control and is acting out of excitement and over-arousal. In contrast, when your dog barks out of the defensive drive, they usually succeed in their intent because their behaviour usually pushes the thing away or they perceive it that way. Every time your dog barks defensively and causes people and dogs to leave the space, the behaviour is reinforced.

If you need to eliminate the barking issue, you must set

your dog up for success by being able to control your dog's movements on your property. Management of your dog's space is essential if they are persistent with barking at prey. For example, you can try and remove the possums by deterring them from your property, or you can allocate a space away from the view of the animals in the time of the day the animals are active. You can do this by separating them into another area of the yard, house or crate at the time when the animals are present.

I advise you to approach the behaviour modification through incremental steps by exposing your dog to the area where they bark while you are around to provide feedback for the behaviour (reward or correction). You should be able to correct and reward appropriately by having a plan on how to correct your dog and what your dog is getting rewarded for. Be clear that you are trying to communicate that barking is undesirable and being quiet is good.

Always use your marker for punishment ('UH-UH') before giving a correction within 1.6 seconds of the behaviour. Have a lead or long lead attached to the collar when your dog is in the area where the barking occurs. Either hold the lead or leave it loose on the ground and have a bed close by to gain some control with training.

Suppose your dog is barking at prey or exciting sounds (not in a conflicted and defensive state), simply 'UH-UH' followed by leash pop. After a few moments, see if your dog re-engages with the stimulus. If your dog looks but doesn't bark, issue recall or bed command. Play or feed your dog to reward the behaviour. If your dog re-engages and barks again, give 'UH-UH'; your dog may stop. If they ignore you, follow through with the leash. If the behaviour decreases over time, leave your dog outside for a little longer each day. Keep a pull tab or 15 cm leash on a dog if you need to follow through with leash pop if your dog does not respond to your punishment marker.

While training and playing with your dog, if your dog keeps disengaging with you to bark at other things, you stop the game and put your dog away in their crate or secure area. You are trying to desensitise your dog to the specific stimulus they are barking at, along with providing an undesirable consequence for barking at the thing.

Sometimes a bark collar is an effective and efficient way to address this type of barking, as it may be late at night or at random times that you cannot personally correct the behaviour.

For barking that is related to predatory drive, the bark collar correction is more successful and understanding to a dog, however a barking collar correction for a defensive/fearful dog can have the opposite effect and confirm the notion that the stimulus is a threat (because the barking collar activated when the dog barked). Refer to the barking collars section for information regarding barking collars.

The best way to advise on eliminating barking defensively at people and dogs walking by your territory is difficult as it relates to your property's distance, layout, geography, location, and how your dog engages with the world around him. Consider your general training and lifestyle with your dog.What are your dog's triggers outside of this barking issue (from your property)? How you maintain and house your dog and most importantly, what is your relationship with your dog? Does your dog respond when you issue commands when they are outwardly focused on other things around them, or is your dog generally nervous about the same triggers when walking?

Your dog is likely calm and quiet, walking by people and dogs on the walk, but behind the fence, they lose their mind. Territorial behaviour is genetic and normal canine behaviour, depending on your dog's past learnt behaviour over the years.

It may be entirely acceptable for your dog to bark when people walk past your fence line and when dogs approach too close to your property, as it is a behaviour that has been specifically bred into most breeds. The security it creates in your home is valuable if you can control it. Most people will not break into a house with a barking dog, big or small; however, this can be very difficult if you live in an apartment block with people walking by constantly.

My dog barks when someone touches the front gate, and I am happy with that. If it goes too long, I can tell him to quiet down and maybe go to his bed. It is ok for some barking, but can your dog listen to you, can you put your dog away when it gets too much, and can you correct it and guide them into better behaviour?

Again, just like most undesirable behaviour, it shows a lack of biological fulfilment in day-to-day life and a strong genetic predisposition to barking. If your dog is barking as a territory behaviour and the potential 'threat' goes away incidental to barking, it is not only reinforced. Still, it is a natural behaviour continuing its expression.

Consider these and put something into practice. If you cannot find a way to manage, train, or find success, you will need to address this with a professional dog trainer in your home, because many variables are at play and are unique to your situation. Most barking, whether it is prey or defence, is best managed by altering your setup and where you contain your dog. Set you and your dog up for success and manage your expectations appropriately.

Barking for attention

If you see your dog standing at the door barking to either let them in or for you to come outside with them, you know your dog is trying to get your attention. This is not referring to separation anxiety. This is a learnt behaviour that your dog understands that their barking is a successful behaviour to get your attention.

Attention-seeking barking is the most common barking issue, and that causes the most stress in some dog owners' lives. It is essential that you understand that the barking is a manifestation of your dog's inability to be calm on its own, and your job is to show that barking will be punished, either by ignoring and removing the dog's access to being inside or by issuing a correction that is undesirable to your dog.

Depending on the time frame and intensity of your dog's barking will determine how quickly you need to stop the behaviour. Usually, the first approach to resolving this issue is ignoring the barking by not letting your dog inside, not talking or looking at your dog. The hardest part is that it will take time, and your dog's barking will go through an extinction burst (see below). Only rewarding or letting your dog inside once they have ceased barking for at least 30-60 seconds will show your dog that barking is not a successful behaviour and being calm and quiet is the behaviour that grants your dog access to be inside.

Practising this daily, it would be a great idea to keep your dog outside while you are home for 30-minute increments, three to four times a day, to develop the habit of being out on their own. Don't make the mistake of creating a 'velcro dog' that follows you everywhere and doesn't know how to be independent. When going out for the day, you want to set your dog up for success to be more comfortable being left alone.

Extinction burst

In psychology, the term extinction refers to the ceasing of behaviour. The behaviour no longer holds any value of reinforcement, which means the behaviour stops occurring. This is often associated with negative punishment and is seen regularly when working through separation distress and attention-seeking behaviours.

If you leave your dog outside in the backyard and close the door, then let your dog inside while barking, you have reinforced the behaviour (stronger and more frequent for the next time).

If, in this example, you wait for your dog to stop barking before letting them come inside, you might find that your dog's behaviour will increase and intensify rapidly to earn the reinforcement (being allowed inside), and this is the 'burst' before the behaviour stops (extinction).

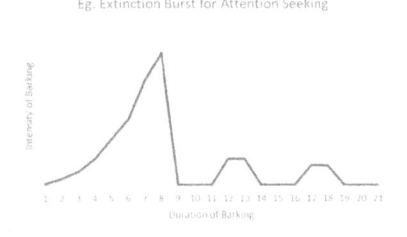

Eg. Extinction Burst for Attention Seeking

Because of this, owners accidentally make the barking a more significant problem over time because people figure their dog is very stressed as the barking manifests into jumping, scratching the door, chewing the door, howling etc., so they let the dog in. This now means more intense behaviour has been reinforced, and your dog will realise what behaviour is successful.

Keep this in mind when trying to eliminate attention-seeking behaviour. If you let your dog inside while the behaviour is on the rise during an extinction burst, wherever on the graph your dog's barking will become the 'successful' behaviour, and the new starting point of the next time you leave them outside.

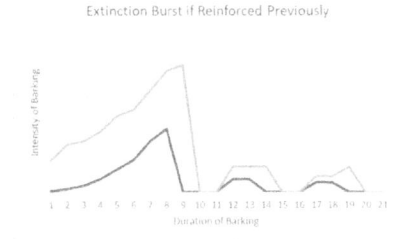

Extinction Burst if Reinforced Previously

The graph above gives an example that if you let your dog in at 'level 50-70', it is likely that your dog starts barking at 'level 50' the next time they are outside on their own as they know that was the successful intensity that granted them access into the house. It only gets more frequent and intense as time and repetitions continue.

It is most desirable to let your dog go through an extinction burst and wait until they are calm and quiet. If you do this from day 1, you will have a dog understand that barking isn't a successful behaviour. Understanding and ignoring extinction bursts is essential to addressing attention-seeking behaviours.

Extinction burst is a phenomenon in other areas of behaviour and is not limited to barking or attention-seeking behaviours. It occurs in animals and humans, too. When past reinforced behaviours suddenly stop, an individual will try the same behaviour harder and more intensely to acquire the intended result. You see s this in humans when waiting to cross the street at traffic lights. If they think they have waited too long, they press the buttons 10 times quickly and harder as though this will change the outcome., Or, when a toddler isn't getting their way and they rapidly intensify a tantrum until they either get what they want or eventually calm down.

Extinction bursts can sometimes be used to help build the intensity of a particular behaviour when reinforced just before the behaviour goes 'extinct'—what owners accidentally do to their barking dog. For example, in improving my dog Nuki's 'MIDDLE' command, I was in the training phase of the middle and rewarding intermittently. I asked her to do the behaviour five times in a row with no reinforcement; usually, I don't ask that many times with no reward for this command. With Nuki's frustration, on the sixth time, I asked her to do the middle command, she performed the behaviour with the very best intensity (frustration builds drive), and I rewarded and jackpotted that behaviour and ended the session there.

Because I have set a new criterion for the middle command, I regularly get that same speed and drive, and I don't reward anything less for that behaviour. If I ask her to do it another two to three more times without rewarding them, I may run the risk of decreasing her drive for that behaviour when I ask her in the following session. If this is the case, I would have to go back and fix it. Where you are with each command will determine the best course of action.

The takeaway from learning about the extinction burst is that we know a behaviour will intensify before it stops, and your dog will try harder than previous times to make the reinforcement occur. Suppose you reinforce your dog at maximum intensity and effort, you will likely get that intensity or close to it for the next repetition. In that case, this can be used in your favour if you get the timing correct. It can also work against you, so observing your dog is key.

Separation distress

Separation distress is when your dog cannot cope with being left alone properly and will bark, whine or display destructive behaviour or attempt to escape.

The difference between separation distress and separation anxiety are listed below. This section covers separation distress, and separation anxiety will be addressed later in this book.

Separation distress: This is a learned behaviour in which the dog has used barking, scratching at the door, and other destructive actions to get what he wants like being let back inside. Giving in reinforces the the unwanted behaviour. Not giving him what he expects creates discomfort and stress which causes him to act out.

Separation anxiety: This is a more severe psychologically and physiologically state and is technically a medical term. The dog is not just uncomfortable or mildly anxious but is experiencing high anxiety levels when left alone. This distinction is vital to know as it determines the training plan necessary.

Separation distress in adult dogs can be a difficult and stressful thing to deal with. It can be caused by recently acquiring a rescue dog, moving to a new house, a change in routines or environment , habits from puppyhood carried over or newly developed behaviour. Wherever they originate, here are ways of resolving this issue.

Some of the techniques and practices that are mentioned below are basic guidelines. Each dog and situation may require a varying method. This can be addressed in further detail in a one-on-one training session with a professional dog trainer.

Before discussing how to remedy your dog's distress when left alone, you must address other indirect causes of why your dog might be experiencing this behaviour. As mentioned throughout this book, it is crucial that you give your dog a job, a purpose, and a way to fulfil their needs daily through both mental and physical stimulation. If we do not give our dogs a job, they will find a way to fulfil those needs; this can manifest in many forms. Separation distress and anxiety can result from not appropriately fulfilling your dog's needs. Ensure that you are providing the appropriate amount of exercise and training your dog needs by following the instructions of what your trainer has given you. Biological fulfilment comes in many forms, depending on your dog's breed, age, temperament & genetics.

Another reason your dog may be distressed when left alone can be because, from a young pup, you have not been proactive in building confidence in being alone. Teach them to spend time independently in the backyard, exercise pen, crate, kennel, or other designated spaces separate from you and the family.

Pups and young dogs that spend 24/7 in the house, sleeping in your bedroom and always around someone will never know how to spend time alone. The lesson here is, give your dog time to spend on their own, build a sense of independence before a problem arises.

If your dog is suffering from separation distress, go for a long, structured walk and practice training session to mentally fulfil your dog before leaving them in your designated area. Provide enrichment in the area you want your dog to be in to keep them entertained and busy.

Teaching your dog to be comfortable with being left alone will take time, patience, and at times frustration. Ensure the location you plan to contain your dog is secure and set yourself up for success. You do not want your dog breaking out of their confined area. This causes further distress, and your dog will become more creative and resilient in trying to get out, which can also cause injury.

The best remedy and tool to address separation distress is by crate training your dog. Crate training will be discussed in detail in chapter 10. There are many ways of dealing with this issue. For example, the dog we will talk about needs to know how to be left alone in the backyard or designated area for a longer duration of time (e.g., 6-8 hours). These steps would apply:

1. Put your dog in the backyard.

2. Start by rewarding immediately (within 5 seconds) with high-value food or your dog's daily food ration. Try to reward before your dog starts to bark, scratch or make noise.

3. Repeat this process for ten repetitions and then let your dog back inside. Only let your dog inside if they are calm and not barking.

4. When your dog is let inside, do not get overexcited and overly praise them. Be calm and ignore until your dog is relaxed.

5. After a bit of rest, take your dog back outside and repeat this process, but this time, increase your duration as appropriate. Usually, I double the increment of time for each jump in the duration of the reward (from 5-10 seconds, 10-20 seconds, 20-40 seconds and so on.)

6. If your dog is barking and making noise, it is best first

to ignore them (do not open the door, tell them to shush or even look at your dog). Wait until they stop barking for the duration you are up to in your training (e.g., 2 minutes) before rewarding or letting your dog back inside or you go outside to your dog. Remember, reinforcement does not only comes in the form of a treat; it is whatever the dog desires at that moment (your attention or presence).

A lot of this advice is very similar to barking issues, except the difference is that real separation distress compared to barking for attention is that separation distress is mild stress. Anxiety disorders can only be diagnosed by a qualified vet, and separation anxiety is overused in the dog world. Anxiety in dogs is genuine; however, just because your dog is uncomfortable with being left alone and barks doesn't always mean your dog is suffering anxiety. Crate training is a beneficial practice and is advised to implement when dealing with separation-related issues.

To conclude this topic, your dog is showing signs of anxiety if it:

- Looks very stressed and cannot settle after a certain amount of time.
- Is displaying extremely distressed behaviour.
- Shows an increase in salivation, is panting, shaking, and pacing consistently.

This is for any time the dog is left alone, whether inside or outside of the house. If these behaviours are consistent then your dog is showing signs of separation anxiety. If your dog is showing signs of distress but can settle with enrichment, demonstrates progress in the training routine.

If you fail to follow this guide, seeking one-on-one professional help is advised. Medication in combination with a behaviour modification plan may sometimes be necessary for extreme cases of anxiety. It is difficult to go into absolute specifics about complex behavioural issues in this book.

I hope this information helps you prevent many problematic issues that can arise and stay consistent from the beginning, which will help your dog understand how to live with you and your family and develop good habits.

Things NOT to do

- Do not respond to your dog's attention while they are barking, this will show your dog that barking is a successful way of getting what they want. Even looking at your dog will reinforce the barking.

- Do not let your dog inside if they are standing at the back door, barking to be allowed inside.

- Do not talk to your dog by saying constructed sentences when they are barking (STOP BARKING, WHAT DO YOU WANT?, etc.). Dogs do not understand English, so you are not successful in stopping their barking. You reward the behaviour by giving the attention your dog wants, but this can desensitise the value of your voice/command or cause confusion and stress to your dog.

Things to do

- Wait at least 10 seconds of quiet behaviour, say 'YES', open the door and REWARD. Do not let your dog inside.

- Repeat this for at least five repetitions before letting your dog inside or you going outside to them.

- Once your dog is good with 10 seconds of not barking, double the duration in increments. (from 10-20 seconds, 20–40 seconds, 40–1 minute, 1-2 minutes, 2–4 minutes, 4-10 minutes, 10-20 minutes, etc.)

- Crate training is a reliable and effective way to help with attention-seeking or separation-related behaviours as it is easier to manage, control and teach your dog how to be calm on their own and limit neighborhood disruptions.

- If you feel they will not stop barking, carefully consider what sort of correction/ punishment is appropriate to eliminate the unwanted behaviour. Specific techniques are best explored in person with a professional dog trainer. However, an option is using a spray bottle and squirting water at your dog when excessive barking occurs. If a spray bottle is not effective, then having your hose ready and giving a quick sharp spray to your dog can work (unless your dog enjoys chasing water from the hose). Before any correction is given, make sure the verbal correction

'UH-UH' comes before the +P.

- Another more uncomplicated technique is with your hand, you can bang the door or gate loudly within 1.6 seconds of unwanted behaviour. Some sensitive dogs will pair their barking with the aversive BANG on the door and avoid barking.

- Remember, when using any form of punishment, you are not endeavouring to hurt, scare or create trauma. You are making a consequence undesirable or uncomfortable for your dog so that it reduces to likelihood or frequency of the behaviour repeating in the future. Do not be angry or frustrated when correcting problem behaviour. Be calm, confident and clear. You are using punishment, not abuse.

- When training with any technique, use as much positive reinforcement as possible to teach your dog WHAT YOU WANT, especially when using punishment to tell your dog what you do not want. You cannot use punishment alone as it is not an effective and appropriate way of training for the longevity of behavioural modification.

- If you have adopted the reinforcement technique only and it works for you, this is excellent. If you find results without punishment, keep doing what you're doing and slowly wean off the rewards over time.

Health issues or injury

You know your dog best, and you will be in tune with what is normal or abnormal behaviour, and it is critical to be aware that sometimes your dog may have a health issue and is barking as a sign of physical distress. It can be challenging to tell if your dog is a nuisance barker or starts to bark because something is wrong, but there is a different type of bark when a dog is in distress.

When a dog experiences an injury, it may bark, or the other dogs may bark to notify you for assistance. This is normal behaviour as dogs are pack animals and communicate these things to the pack. It's a natural response to run to your dog's aid when you hear a distressing bark. The lesson here is to acknowledge and be aware of your dog's patterns of behaviour.

Barking collars

Barking collars are the last line of defence in stopping our dogs from barking. They are a very effective tool but can be purchased unnecessarily for barking that can be controlled in other ways. Barking collars come in many varieties and can be a pricey purchase to try the different options.

The collars can be very effective as the timing of the correction (either a spray, electric stimulation or vibration) is directly issued to the dog immediately after the collar detects the bark. You do not need to be a part of the correction, and you do not need to be anywhere close to the barking; therefore, it is a very reliable tool.

If you have been advised to use a barking collar or have already purchased one to eliminate your dog's barking, there are a few things you will need to do for the most effective outcome.

Make sure that whichever barking collar you decide to use for your dog that the collar will simultaneously detect both the sound and the vibration of your dog's neck when barking, ensuring your dog is being corrected ONLY from their own barking and not other sounds. If you get a collar that only detects sound, it will likely malfunction and spray when the collar is bumped against something or detects another dog's bark (that is not wearing the collar).

Introducing a barking collar to your dog:

1. Put the barking collar on your dog, and make sure it is turned OFF.

2. Do this for a few days for 30 minute increments while you go for a walk, feed dinner, play, etc.

3. When it is time to turn the collar on, put another flat collar on that your dog has not ever seen or worn before, and at the same time, you turn the collar ON.

4. When it is time to turn the barking collar OFF, take off the new collar.

5. Repeat this process for at least 1-2 weeks; this will condition the dog to associate any corrections they received with the new flat collar, not the barking collar. This will allow you to not rely on the barking collar, as the new flat collar is what your dog thinks will create the correction when they bark. This new flat collar can stay on your dog as their new flat collar.

6. Be careful with using a bark collar because if your dog is barking out of anxiety or fear, you may create a bigger problem as your dog's fear or anxiety may get worse. Also, if you require your dog to bark at some things but not others, you may deter your dog from barking when you want them to.

   For example, if you want your dog to bark when people approach the front gate but have been punishing the dog for barking with a bark collar in other circumstances, they may not bark to alert you that someone is on the property or be conflicted and stressed.

   Another thing to be mindful of is if your dog is barking as a fear response to certain stimuli. When the dog is punished via bark collar, the stimulation from the collar may create a worse association with the stimuli that elicited the fear response. These are things to consider before using barking collars.

7. Make sure that if you choose to use a bark collar, it is alongside the advice and technique shared earlier. Reinforcing desirable behaviour and a good management plan is essential, not just the collar on its own. The barking collar is a tool, not a quick fix, and must be used in conjunction with a training plan as described.

Diary for neighbours

The biggest issue for our dog's barking is for our neighbours, and it can be a quick way of creating a bad relationship with them. Instead of arguing or ignoring each other, which can result in receiving council warnings and fines, it is best to try and work with your neighbours as much as you can.

Since they are the ones that hear most of your dog's barking when you are not home, I have found providing them with a table that they can mark when they hear barking that last more than 5 minutes.

They fill it out to give you the information needed to address the behaviour and correct it. It also allows you to be the point of contact concerning your dog's barking (share a phone number or email address), so your neighbour does not need to contact the council as their first contact. Work together, as it is in everyone's best interest to stop your dog from barking and being a nuisance to the community.

Some products, such as pet cameras and security systems, have options for you to watch your dog via an app, which can also send notifications to alert you that your dog has been barking. These notifications can be saved as a log for you, which can be used as evidence of whether it was your dog or what time your dog was barking. This can be very helpful for proving to strata, council, or neighbours whether it was your dog causing the nuisance.

The log is also useful for tracking how your dog has been doing, whether they have been improving and whether barking has decreased.

AN EXAMPLE FOLLOWS OF WHAT THE TABLE CAN LOOK LIKE. **X** MEANS THE DOG BARKED FOR MORE THAN 5 MINUTES. FILL IN THE HOURS APPROPRIATE TO WHEN YOU WILL BE

OUT OF THE HOUSE AND HAVE ALL THE DAYS OF THE WEEK ON THE TABLE.

	MON	TUES	WED	THURS
8AM				
8:30AM		X		
9AM				X

BED in function

The BED command is one of the most practical commands when your dog is in your home. Your home should not be a playground for your dog. You should have control over your dog when in your personal space to encourage a calm environment.

The BED command is a controlled position for your dog to stay in their 'bed' until released with a verbal command. The steps for teaching, training and proofing the BED command is in the chapter covering commands.

This skill of remaining in one spot has many benefits for both short- and long-term use and can be used in many situations. To send your dog to stay in bed shows a level of impulse control, and the ability to go to a target location away from you is convenient in providing a spot for your dog that is in a suitable area. The bed can be moved anywhere and still be a functional and convenient command.

At my place and in many of my client's homes, the dogs are allowed inside but must have a solid understanding of what the command means.

Like with most of the commands we train, we want to practice and make behaviours habitual, so when you need them, you have them.

Here are some examples that show how we use the BED command in function in daily life:

- When visitors come over, and they have a small child still learning how to act around dogs, I send them to their bed so that they are calm and relaxed. Even though my dogs are very social and friendly, they may be overwhelming to small children. This is also for visitors that may not be comfortable around dogs or if your dog tends to get too excited around people.

- Dog owners struggle to have dinner with their dog around because the dog is barking, jumping or doing other attention-seeking behaviour for the food they have on the table. We teach the dog to stay on the bed in that area. The bed becomes a 'feeding station'; they learn that the longer they remain there, the more food they receive. Over time, you should be able to send your dog to bed without food or a reward to follow. In the early stages, you reward frequently.

- I have used the BED command at the vet, given the command 'BED', and my dog walks onto the scales for me to weigh him.

- If I am at a friend's house or the beach, I put a towel, small blanket or even a t-shirt on the floor and command BED. This is an excellent tool for management and control. My dogs are happy to be on their bed, which is familiar and straightforward. Best to tell your dog where to be rather than focusing on where not to be.

- An example of how I use my bed command was when I was at a dog event. I had a stall set up and my dogs (Chilli & Nuki) with me. While I engaged with people and their dogs, I sent them to their beds in the shade out of the way, and they stayed there until I released them. There were 100 s of people and their dogs that day in a bustling environment, and my two dogs stayed on their beds for up to and over 45 minutes at a time. I still rewarded them intermittently to reinforce their efforts, especially when people let their dogs get too close. This is a handy and safe practice that helped my job that day.

There are many more examples. As you make this ritual for your dog, it will become something you can use in many situations. If your dog is wild in your home, start with having your dog on the lead, and make small training sessions of the BED command.

Over time you will increase Distance, Duration and add Distraction throughout the training and proofing of this behaviour. Baby steps to success rather than giant leaps of failure. Of course, as always, set you and your dog up for success, manage the space you are training appropriately and be consistent.

Leaving your dog inside

Leaving a dog inside unattended inside and outside of your

home when you leave for work or go to sleep at night should come with a level of trust, time, and experience. Most people give their dog too much freedom too soon. This results in the dog earning less freedom over time, as they lose access due to their behaviour. Your dog should learn through everyday living how to behave in the house and respect and follow the rules/ boundaries you have set up.

I can leave my dogs in my house for a full day without any destructive behaviour or toileting issues. This is because, over time, I have given them more freedom once they learn how to follow the rules. In my current circumstances, my dogs sleep outside and spend most of the day outside. They are inside when we are home and chilling out. There are days when it's too hot or cold, so they spend a longer period inside, even left unattended.

If you are comfortable and confident to leave your dog inside unattended, make sure that you have assessed their behaviour while you are home and present. Ensuring that they follow all the rules you have set up, whether that's no jumping on a couch or bed unless invited, no toileting in the house, no destructive behaviour, and no anxious behaviour.

To this day, I still won't leave a cupcake on the coffee table with my dog unattended as I know it will get eaten, so I make sure I don't allow it to happen. Even a trained dog will be tempted and may try to push the boundaries. Always ensure that no hazardous items or substances are lying around and that you proof the things you like most to prevent damage.

Be sure to:

- Give your dog access to an outside or toileting spot.

- Take your dog out to the toilet before leaving.

- Proof the area in the house.

- Ensure they can spend 1 hour successfully on their own before trying three or even six hours immediately.

My general advice is to contain your dog appropriately when left unattended. I have heard and witnessed many issues when dogs have ultimate freedom in the home, which results in injury and sometimes death! If dogs get stuck in a dangerous position, swallow an item, or get their head stuck in an empty bag of chips, these horrible things can happen, so be mindful.

It's not a defeat if your dog cannot spend time in your home with absolute freedom to do as they please. Some dogs are capable, and others not, depending on how you set up your space, living situation, experience, and the dog's needs. Keeping dogs in their secure area (backyard, crate, kennel, courtyard, or pen/run) is always advised. This is a guide for you. You also know your dog best and knowing all the factors contributing to being left alone inside and being intuitively self-guided plays a role. If in doubt, don't risk it. Safety first!

Door etiquette

Many people struggle when someone is at the front door, and you must let your visitor in. Your dog may be jumping, barking, lunging, trying to run through the opening gap of the door, etc.

It would be best if you had control over your dog when at any doorway for several essential reasons:

- **Safety:** Dogs run onto the road more times than I like to hear, resulting in injury or death. If your dog is secure inside, they cannot be hit by a car. You may have a 'reliable recall', but best not to practice with your dog's life or the safety of your guests that walk through the front door.

- If your dog is bouncing off children or the elderly, it causes significant issues, including creating a trip hazard when entering or exiting doorways. Bad habits result in unforeseen drama, so safety is always the priority.

- **Over-excitement:** If you cannot regulate your dog's excitement and struggle with your dog's lack of impulse control while people are coming through the door, you will have an annoying, unsettled and possibly dangerous situation that may unfold. Most people like dogs, but most people do not want to be jumped on uninvited, slobbered on, scratched, ruined/dirty clothing and pushed around by your dog (even if they are small and cute). It is just rude and unacceptable to not be able to control your dog while people are coming over to visit.

- **Practicality:** Have clear and concise communication and establish a routine when people come over. You want to master your castle and control your dog in all situations, especially when people enter your house. It is impractical to hold your dog back by the collar, pick them up and try to catch them to take them into your backyard when people come over. Frustrating!

What to do at the door

There are a few variations of what to do at the door, either when walking in/out or allowing guests to come in/out.

You want to teach your dog from the beginning that they can only move through the front door if told to. Also, it helps if you have a door that automatically shuts. The less opportunity your dog gets to run through the front door, the better. A dog successfully barging out through the front door reinforces disruptive behaviour. The dog not only gets access to the world, scent, people, dogs, and cats, but also the fun game of you chasing and bribing with food to come back inside!

The more you allow your dog to rehearse this behaviour, the more likely and frequent it will become. Good management includes self-closing doors and gates, especially openings giving access to public and dangerous places such as the road, people, and other dogs.

It is important that visitors are not ruining your training when they come over. No pats or attention for jumping; no over-excited screaming or talking that will excite your dog; and no treats for behaviour you don't want to reinforce. Your visitors must be calm and practice no talk, no touch and no eye contact only until the dog is calm and your guests have entered your space. After that, pat the dog for calm and appropriate behaviour.

These impulse control techniques surrounding the door will become a way of life, a ritual your dog will follow, making it easier and minimising anxiety or out-of-control behaviour when opening the door.

'BED' command near the door by doing the following:

1. Only start when you are in the training phase of the 'BED' command.

2. Have your dog on a lead and place the bed (doormat or small rug) around 3 meters from the door.

3. 'BED' and walk a couple of steps toward the door. 'YES' + REWARD + 'OK' to release off the bed and praise.

4. If your dog gets up, 'UH-UH' and take your dog back to the bed by their lead/collar. DO NOT repeat the 'BED' command.

5. Do this progressively get closer to the door (may take a few sessions).

6. Once your dog stays on the bed for 10-20 seconds while you wait near the door, tap the door handle (usually the sound of the handle excites the dog, and they may release themselves off their bed. If your dog stayed on the bed, 'YES' + REWARD or release.

7. As your dog stays on the bed, repeat the steps, and now add the door opening and gradually extend the

time the door is opened while your dog successfully stays on the bed while the door is opened.

8. Over time, you can walk in and out of the door, and your dog will stay in bed until it is released 'OK'.

9. The next step will be practising this while people are at the door. It will take time, but consistency and patience will pay off in the long term. You will have more success if you have the lead attached to your dog to set you all up for a good outcome.

10. Don't skip a step. Your dog should perform behaviour 10/10 until they progress to the next stage in your criteria. Give your dog what it needs to meet this goal, and be clear as possible.

BED in function- Stop dog running out the door

https://me-qr.com/nO1UgIoK

Claim the door:

1. When your guests are on the other side of the door, and your dog is bouncing up and down on the door, you must get in between your dog and the door and face your dog.

2. Firmly walk into your dog (spacial pressure) until your dog is at least 1-2 meters away from the door. Be persistent; your dog will try to run around you, so you must stand your ground. Be assertive and calm, do not be frustrated and angry.

3. You can control your dog with a leash on, but practising this without the leash is practical to achieve the same result with your body language, which will be helpful for everyday normal living (no leash on in the house).

4. As you are doing this, you will notice that your dog will look up at you. Sometimes your dog may naturally sit, or you can command 'SIT' as soon as they do, 'YES' + REWARD.

5. Remember your dog needs to stay in a SIT until you release 'OK'.

6. When you turn around, your dog may continue to run up to the door; if so, repeat until your dog is back in that position away from the door.

7. You need that buffer zone/bubble so when you let your visitors in, they don't walk on top of your dog, or your dog can't run out the front door.

8. Other techniques will be shown throughout this book on how to stop your dog from jumping on people, but remember, when people come in, and your dog is showing desirable behaviour, 'YES' + REWARD (even if the treat comes from your guest).

9. If you know your dog will jump on your visitors, you should have a leash attached before visitors approach the door.

10. Using the BED command is also applicable, but establishing boundaries around doorways is a life skill, and one must have this level of control and communication without relying on a BED or a leash.

Set a boundary:

1. Establish an area around the door where your dog is not allowed when people are entering/exiting the door.

2. It can be an area outlined by certain tiles, an invisible line from the closest door near the front door or a part of the corridor leading to the front door. You can put tape down as a physical boundary if that helps you and the family remain consistent.

3. You may use either the BED command or claim your space by using special pressure to move your dog out of the 'buffer zone' around the door. This offers better control when around the door but also gives your dog a clear understanding of what is expected without necessarily expressing what not to do.

4. Instead, you're telling your dog what you want from them, which will be easier for your dog to follow.

5. It is better to try and stop your dog from moving into a buffer zone/bubble than to stop them from running

through the doorway.

Spatial pressure- Stopping dog out the door

https://me-qr.com/aFYSpQq7

Doorbell

To minimise the intensity of your dog acting crazy when the doorbell rings, you can practice a few things to create a different response to the doorbell ringing. It is essential to understand that it may be complicated to completely desensitise a dog to the sound of the doorbell, especially if it is a behaviour and a conditioned response over a long period.

You want to desensitise your dog to the sound of the doorbell. Dogs bark excessively when the doorbell goes off because it stimulates excitement when people come over or can create territorial behaviour.

The doorbell is an excellent example of classical conditioning. Your dog's mind/body is experiencing people at the door (thought, feeling, chemical release) just by the doorbell sound (condition stimulus). The behaviour (conditioned response) of barking has been reinforced for many repetitions, which is why it is challenging to eliminate.

The behaviour is reinforced in many different ways, usually because your dog's barking has been rewarded by the presence of your visitors entering your house. Getting patted, spoken to and played with is highly reinforcing to a dog that likes people.

To make this training successful do the following:

- Replace the current doorbell or change the tune it plays so that you can create a new conditioned response to a new stimulus.

- Purchase a wireless doorbell from a local hardware store with two separate buttons.

- Attach one button to the front door and the other on you.

- Set the doorbell to a different tone, entirely unlike the current sound. The goal is to associate a new sound with a new behaviour in your dog.

- Ring the doorbell that you have on you while you are inside the house, 'YES' + REWARD within 1.6 seconds of your dog hearing the new doorbell. Repeat this process and give a substantial amount of food.

- Make sure your dog does not see you pressing the doorbell. Have it in your pocket, on somebody else, or out of your dog's sight.

- Once you notice your dog focused on you when they hear the doorbell, it is time to make your dog's bed the place to go whenever the doorbell rings.

- Put an extra bed (floor mat) within three metres of the door.

- Press the bell and immediately give your dog the command 'BED', wait 5-10 seconds, then release and reward.

- Add walking to the door between command and release command.

- Practise these steps until your dog associates the doorbell with the bed command. Once you see a less intense reaction to the sound of the bell, you are ready for the following steps.

- Making an influential association with this new doorbell means food is available when the dog goes to their bed, and your dog will focus more on you and the unique ritual when the doorbell rings.

- This process is called counter-conditioning which is further explained in the behaviour modification chapter.

Recall in and out of the door:

- Your dog must be in the training phase of their 'COME' recall command and should understand either the 'BED' command near the door and where the boundary is surrounding the front doorway.

- Have your dog on a 10 m-long lead.

- Have your dog in the desired position inside and walk

outside with the door opened.

- Call 'COME' (while still holding the lead) and reward when your dog comes to you.

- I recommend letting the dog spend about a minute outside to sniff around, etc., and while they are doing that, walk inside and recall your dog again, reward if your dog comes back.

- If your dog does not come back, put pressure on the long lead to encourage your dog to come. If they are too focused on something else, reel in the lead to correct for not complying with the command.

- You must practice this regularly and follow the recall command's training/proofing phase steps through the doorway. Hoping your dog never runs out the front door won't keep it from happening. Your recall is an important command and must be reliable, so practice often, as it may save your dog's life!

9
General Manners

Jumping

Dogs jumping up on people is one of the most common behaviours asked in training consultations. Most of the time it's caused by excitement and previous reinforcement of that specific behaviour. If you pat your dog, move, turn your back, or talk to them when they jump up on you, you reinforce the behaviour, increasing the likelihood of it occurring the following time.

The good old advice of 'ignoring' and turning away from the dog rarely proves to be successful—maybe effective with very young, medium-energy pups. Its ineffectiveness is because you're responding to the jumping by moving away and turning around, and your dog will follow you and continue the behaviour as if it is a game. It is an oxymoron to say ignore (do nothing) and turn away (do something), so the advice of ignoring your dog and turning your back to them usually doesn't work.

Instead, it is more effective to address the undesirable behaviour by issuing a form of correction or undesirable outcome due to your dog's jumping. There are two different types of jumping, either on you or other people. If your dog is jumping on you, it is usually different advice than if your dog jumps on somebody else who is not responsible, skilled, or wanting to correct your dog for jumping.

Jumping on you

If your dog is jumping on you, you must walk into your dog's space by literally walking into them with high knees (don't knee or kick your dog). Say 'UH-UH' and walk firmly into your dog while raising your knees. You immediately stop walking into their space as soon as your dog stops jumping. You can pat your dog with medium-level energy if all four paws are on the floor. You may need to follow your dog up for up to a few seconds until your dog calms down and sees that her jumping is being interrupted and discouraged. Be calm and assertive with this, do not talk to your dog and give commands; just body language on its own. Sharing these instructions can be challenging to tell visitors to do as they walk into your house.

Jumping on guests

If your dog likes to jump on your visitors, as mentioned, it is not their job to stop your dog from jumping, and they have no idea what you're telling them to do while they have to deal with your dog jumping up all over them. It is as simple as attaching a lead to your dog's collar. You can hold the lead or have the lead loose on the floor. Once you see your dog loading her back legs ready to jump, issue the verbal punishment marker 'UH-UH' and follow up immediately with leash correction (pop on the lead). If your dog responds and stops jumping, you can tell your visitor to walk inside and interact with the dog when they are calm, or if they choose not to engage with your dog, that is also okay. If someone wants to pat your dog, they must be sitting to receive the visitor's affection.

The BED command is handy in this situation. However, it is necessary to communicate and train your dog to understand that jumping on people is unacceptable and will be corrected immediately. This is the beauty of good management; you can set your situation up for success, which means your dog learns faster and has more freedom in your house quicker as they know the rules of engagement when spending time with people.

Be consistent and firm immediately and address the undesirable jumping. This behaviour is annoying, rude, destructive (it can hurt and ruin clothing), scary to some people, and dangerous, particularly for children and older people. Be clear about what your dog is supposed to do; teach her how to greet people appropriately and develop her impulse control using the following steps:

1. As soon as your dog jumps up on you, walk into their space firmly.

2. When all four paws are on the floor, 'YES' + REWARD.

3. Do not pat or excite your dog for jumping on you, it will reinforce the behaviour.

4. When coming home, be calm and greet your dog when they are relaxed. Building appropriate behaviours while they are young is good etiquette.

5. When visitors come over, instruct them to ignore your

dog (no touch, no talk, no eye contact) until you tell them it is okay to greet them. Ensure they are calm when greeting your dog. Get your friends to 'YES' + REWARD for all four paws on the floor.

6. Keeping your dog on a lead when visitors first come over can help control the jumping if you know your dog does jump on people. Management and control are number one, so be proactive.

7. If your dog jumps on someone, firmly correct them with a sharp, firm pop on the lead. Continue to reward them when they have all four paws on the floor.

8. Also, practice bed command as part of the rules when people come over to maintain control and develop appropriate etiquette.

9. Put your dog in their crate, backyard, or secure area when you are unable to manage the situation. Bring your dog out when you can effectively control him, so they don't rehearse jumping as a fun game. Your friends may not care if your dog jumps on them, which means they may reinforce the behaviour and undo your training.

Mouthing and nipping

Mouthing: Whole mouth and teeth on hands and limbs but not hard enough to puncture the skin, usually exhibited when teething, initiating play, or playing, can also be a learnt behaviour for attention seeking that wasn't addressed in puppyhood, and some breeds are mouthier than others.

Mouthing is more like wrestling energy.

Nipping: When a dog displays small mini bites, usually using its front teeth, usually to initiate play, or when a dog is overexcited and starts nipping to get a reaction or can't help it (lack of impulse control), it can be a symptom of a learnt behaviour as well. Nipping is different to mouthing as it is short sharp 'jabs'.

Biting: I classify biting as an intentional or reflexive behaviour either displayed as a defensive/ aggressive behaviour or a predatory behaviour to catch something. Aggressive behaviour will be covered in a later chapter.

There is a difference between these three, and it is essential to make this distinction as it changes the approach needed to eliminate undesirable behaviour.

If your dog is no longer teething (typically over six months old) and is still mouthing or nipping your hands, legs and clothing, you must stop this behaviour as soon as possible. Identify when your dog is likely to put her teeth on you, generally due to either over-arousal when playing, first coming home or when the dog wants something (food, play or attention).

A lot of the time, this is typical and expected behaviour and is not learnt but was never discouraged in puppyhood. Other times, it's a learnt behaviour, and you have indirectly trained your dog to jump and mouth on you as they know it is a predictable behaviour that results in fun.

First, to address this behaviour, do not encourage mouthing on your body or clothing. Set yourself and your dog up for success by knowing when he's likely to start mouthing and nipping (don't wear nice clothes or loose jewellery). Attach lead and collar to the dog, and practise the impulse control technique game.

While playing the game, if your dog decides to grab your arm, a correction via the leash at that moment can be effective. Don't stop the game, but be clear that the correction is for mouthing and nipping. Continue to reward efforts of obedience while playing (sit, down, bed, etc.) and teach your dog that if they get too excited, they are not allowed to bite you but need to do something else instead.

If your dog is inclined to mouth and nip when overly excited, they will likely enjoy the tug game. In a structured training session, give your dog an appropriate outlet for using its mouth and teeth.

With this concept, along with impulse control, reward and correction, you should be able to play freely with your dog while being clear about what you like and do not like. The goal is to play freely with your dog while communicating and maintaining a healthy respect for the game and interaction.

If mouthing is extreme and you need the lead attached the whole time you are together, so be it. For the short term, this is okay. Put your dog in the crate or the backyard when you feel they are overtired or being too painful; this sort of time out can work as soon as they mouth you, and also, putting your dog away as you see her behaviour leads to a mouthy and nippy state. Don't overexcite your dog, and be prepared for jumping, barking and mouthing.

Know your dog, meet halfway, and have the right

expectations. This is why the BED command is helpful, along with good management as always; know your dog's habits and set a plan accordingly.

Other ways of correcting mouthing if no leash is attached to your dog are difficult to explain in writing; however, a quick firm poke to the side of the dog's rib before removing them by getting a hold of their collar. Ensure you follow through after any correction. The pop or poke snaps your dog's mind out of the behaviour, your following through is the consequence.

Digging

Dogs dig holes for a few different reasons. It is an instinctive behaviour that wild dogs and related canine species do; they dig a hole to lay in to keep warm in colder months and stay cool in warmer months.

The dogs that live with us don't usually dig holes to keep warm or cool as we have generally tended to those needs. It is because of other reasons that our dogs dig and mess up our beautiful backyards.

Common reasons for dogs digging holes are boredom and lack of physical and mental stimulation/exercise, which develops into a habit. Some other less common reasons for digging are that dogs can hear and smell creepy crawlies in the ground, like worms and other bugs and choose to eat or play with them or they dig holes to get under a fence line to escape the yard. Once you know your dog's digging habits, you can combat the issue and seek a solution much easier.

Things you must do to minimise or eliminate digging:

- **Safety first.** Ensure your yard is fully secure and that there is no way your dog can dig under the fence line. I suggest either digging a trench under all boundary fence lines and installing a timber sleeper (at least 20-30 cm wide), pouring fresh concrete in the trench or adding wide pavers under the fence line. If your dog is to dig, they need to dig very deep to escape the yard. In my experience, these above options are enough to keep your dog in the yard.

- **Protect.** If you find your dog lying in the hole they dug for comfort, then ensure they are protected from the elements appropriately, and ensure they are warm when it's cold or cool when it's warm. You can provide a kennel for your dog to sleep in, a jumper on your dog in winter, good coverage from sun and wind, enough water, or set up a mini pool (fill shell-shaped kids pool with water).

- **Stimulate.** If your dog is digging out of boredom and needs extra stimulation, make sure you are walking daily, training sessions, multiple short sessions, and providing enrichment. These points are made clear through this book regarding dogs needing a job/purpose, mind-body exercise, and ways to fulfil their needs daily. If we don't provide an outlet and a way for our dogs to release pent-up energy and frustration, then it may manifest into digging and other undesirable behaviours. Digging is a problem, but the solution isn't always about addressing digging; it's finding its cause and dealing with a holistic solution.

- **Break the habit.** Ways of breaking the digging habit. Fill up one of those kids' shell pools/sandpits with river sand, and make sure you drill holes in the bottom so that water can drain out when it rains. Hide some treats on top and 1 cm under the sand. Over time as your dog starts finding the treats, you gradually hide the food (or a couple of KONG™ toys filled with high-value food inside) deeper inside the sand pit. This will encourage your dog to dig into that particular spot to receive tasty treats and leave the other areas alone.

  Make sure that you cover all holes as soon as you find them. Best to even out the area with soil that has been dug out and try to save some of the grass. You may need a couple of spare bags of topsoil in the shed to fill the holes. Cover the hole with a firm mesh or section off with pegs and chicken wire, and water the area to get the grass growing back. If we cover and maintain the yard, it always looks like how we want it to our dog. If you leave it, your yard will have landmines everywhere. This is unsafe and looks messy, encouraging further digging.

- **Correct immediately.** If you punish the digging, it must be done at the moment (within 1.6 seconds of the behaviour). A few ways to punish could be to use verbal correction ('UH-UH') because this verbal correction is used when your dog is on the lead and is associated with a leash correction, it communicates to your dog that they have done the wrong thing. Following through by removing your dog from the area, you can use the hose if your dog does not enjoy getting sprayed to the head. This is a less invasive way of correcting this behaviour and gives you distance as you can project water meters away. Do not try to punish in any way after the 1.6-second time frame, your dog will not know why they are being punished.

Other things that can work to discourage digging include the following:

- Put your dog's poop in the holes to deter your dog from continuing to dig.

- I once put an inflated balloon in a hole and covered it with soil, the dog dug the hole, and the balloon popped into her face, which stopped the behaviour. This does not always work, but it may be worth a try.

- Cayenne pepper in the digging areas has worked before but has not always been successful. You can also think of other natural and safe deterrents like vinegar or store-bought repellants. Not a very reliable method, but it has worked with some dogs over the years.

- Alternatively, with adequate fencing, you can section your dog into a specific part of the yard. Keep your dog in a space where you allow your dog to play and live while other valued areas of the yard are untouched. You can allow access to the rest of the yard while supervised, but when your dog is alone, they stay in the designated area. Management is always critical and should always be addressed if you want to be successful. .

- Providing enrichment is essential to dogs that are digging holes in the yard.

Destructive behaviour

Destructive behaviour is a similar issue to digging. It is a natural behaviour especially prevalent in puppyhood. It can still be an issue in dogs up to three years old, even though all dogs of all ages chew and destroy things we like. Usually caused by boredom and habit, it is a fun pastime for dogs to fulfil their desire to bite, chew and kill things. Dogs are predators that use their mouths to dismember prey, so destructive behaviour can be linked to this instinctive trait and, thus, is a natural behaviour that should be expected.

As mentioned, and always worth repeating, you must physically and mentally fulfil your dog's needs daily! Your dog's pent-up energy will manifest into destructive behaviour, including your furniture, rugs, personal items, couch, doors, carpets, shoes, and so on.

Appropriate management and living arrangements must be addressed, especially if your dog has been destroying things you value. This is essential, especially for apartment living, as you are limited to space for your dog to live.

A great piece of advice I received is that dogs should be crated or in their yard, balcony, dog run, etc., every time left alone until a year old and never left unattended inside your personal space until age two. The importance of this is that we are never letting our dogs do something we don't want them to do, and when sharing the space with us, your dog should be supervised. Crating can be beneficial in many ways and must be considered to resolve the issue.

Destructive behaviour is not only an undesirable habit because our personal belongings have sentimental and financial value, but it can be potentially life-threatening to your dog. They could accidentally swallow something, get their head or part of their body stuck inside something, or escape your property.

If you do not decide to crate train your dog, then set up an area for your dog to be safe and free from valuable items, furniture or particular parts of the property. This can be a fenced-off area within the yard, part of an outdoor courtyard/balcony, a kennel/outdoor run, etc.

Things you can try to discourage and eliminate destructive behaviour:

- Providing enrichment is essential to dogs that have destructive behaviour issues. Allow your dog to destroy the items you want them to. Make it fun and fulfilling, better than destroying the things you like.

- Control what your dog has access to when supervised and unsupervised. Don't leave your favourite shoes on the floor where your dog can chew them. If you are going to take a shower, put your dog in the allocated area, do not leave it unattended before they are ready to be trusted. When they are in the house, practice the bed command.

- Keeping your dog in a designated area is suitable for other applications, too. If your dog is hard to control inside your house, keep them on a lead for maximum control.

- Adequate exercise and mental stimulation daily. Biological fulfilment creates calm, well-mannered dogs.

- Use deterrents like deep heat cream, vinegar, or store-bought bitter-taste deterrents applied to hard surfaces (wooden furniture, doors, etc.). This works because when your dog puts their mouth on the item or furniture, they find the smell and taste undesirable and stop the unwanted behaviour. Make sure you only apply a little at first. You don't want the dog to consume it. If your dog is consuming the product, stop using it immediately.

- If you choose to punish destructive behaviour, it must be done immediately (within 1.6 seconds of the behaviour). A few ways to punish could be to use verbal correction ('UH-UH') because this verbal correction is used when your dog is on the lead and is associated with a leash correction. It communicates to your dog that they have done the wrong thing.

- Following through with a leash correction or firm

touch to the side of their ribs and removing your dog from the area is most important so that they learn they have lost the privilege of being inside your home. Do not try to punish in any way after the 1.6-seconds time frame because your dog will not know why they are being punished.

10
Management is Key to Success

I have learned over the last decade from other dog trainers across the globe that management is critical to achieving your dog training goals.

If you fail to plan, you plan to fail. This is true because you must plan, prepare and have management strategies to succeed in your training and your dog's overall behaviour. If you wish to eliminate certain behaviours your dog displays or have expectations of how you like your dog to behave, then make sure you have as much control as possible, especially in the early days of bringing your pup/dog into your home. You can never control the environment, but you can control what you do. he more you set processes in place, the more you can rely on them in preparation for when situations and behaviours change or don't go to plan.

Know your dog's patterns of behaviour and set up the environment or your activity according to your training goals. If your dog pees in the same spot of the house when you have a shower, then put your dog in the backyard or other designated area when you leave the space or home. The more your dog pees in the spot you don't like, the habit remains and strengthens; however, while you are present, you can see your dog's cues to guide them to the correct behaviour or catch your dog in the act and provide a consequence.

If, for example, your dog is aggressive to people coming into your house, having a management plan is essential! The thing to do in this situation is have your dog contained in a secure area or crate. When you are exercising, walking, or out of the secure area while people are present, have your dog on the lead and muzzled. These management plans are crucial in training, behaviour modification, and setting your dog up for success.

This idea of good management is one of the main foundational pieces to your dog's life. Whether you are living/training/interacting with a puppy, an adult dog or a dog with behaviour issues, it still applies to your responsibility as a dog owner. Management isn't only about controlling your dog's physical body (controlled areas) and puppy-proofing your house (also for adult dogs) to avoid destructive and inappropriate behaviour. Other examples of good management include having treats handy in different locations you are likely going to be with your dog (home, car, etc.), making sure you are entering environments where the dog is confident, not overwhelming them with stimuli more than your dog can deal with, and having good situational awareness of both what is occurring around you and how your dog is reacting to these things.

The best way to avoid behavioural issues is to start your training journey and knowledge of dog behaviour as early as possible. If you have just acquired an older dog with issues or problem behaviour, set up their world to suit you and your dog. Management first, then rehabilitation can follow, which is key to the power of these concepts. It will save you and your dog stress and energy. This is a fundamental element to all of your training. Many areas of this book pragmatically give management examples, depending on what is being discussed.

Using the right tools

If your trainer has allocated you specific training equipment (i.e., leads, collars, treat pouch, muzzle), ensure you use it consistently and correctly at all times. If you have been issued a slip lead, for example, you must have your dog wearing it correctly, high on their neck (under the jaw and behind the ears) & ensuring it is on the correct way, (refer to equipment section). This is every single time the leash is attached to your dog's collar, not just for training walks. BE CONSISTENT!

Too often, owners start consistently and get great results but then taper off after 30 days and return to old habits. If your dog responds to food with high drive and you know it will help with focus-building techniques when out and about, but you do not have a pouch with food, you are wasting a great opportunity to further your training.

Taking the training seriously and having a committed approach will allow you to see results much faster and longer lasting. This is for safety and to ensure you have the tools to communicate clearly to your dog.

Leashes must be of high quality, especially for larger, powerful breeds. If you choose cheap products, you are more likely to experience equipment failure by leashes, collars and harnesses breaking, which is an avoidable disaster waiting to happen. Cheap long leads tend to fail the most frequently as dogs run and build momentum where the buckle or material snaps and dogs run away.

Having the right tool is essential, and knowing how to use it appropriately is most important.

Crate training

Crate training your dog can be a beneficial thing to teach from as early as possible with your dog for many reasons. When taught correctly, you will have the ability to send your dog into the crate for a certain period which significantly helps with the following:

- Management

- House training (avoiding toilet training & destructive behaviour issues)

- Separation distress/anxiety

- Transportation & travel

- Security

Once your dog is appropriately trained to spend time in the crate, it creates 'conditioned relaxation'. This is where being inside the crate creates a conditioned response to be calm and relaxed because nothing exciting occurs inside the crate, and it is a consistently calm place for your dog to spend independently. It is essential that the first encounter with the crate is a positive one, so your dog will accept it and be comfortable enough to go into the crate and remain for a certain period without experiencing stress and anxiety.

People with a young puppy or new dog in the household will benefit from crate training significantly as it allows you to manage your dog appropriately for the time that you are not going to be able to supervise them. A dog cannot destroy the contents of your home/apartment if they are securely inside of a crate, ensuring that the crate is the correct material and strength for the dog.

I prefer metal crates that are strong enough for the dog not to be able to break out of it by bending the bars or breaking the door. Securing your dog inside a metal secure crate allows you to ensure it is safe and not ingesting the incorrect material (garbage, cords, carpet, furniture, etc.) along with the dangers of injury trying to escape from the actual crate itself.

Dogs do not like to eliminate where they eat or sleep. This is another reason why the crate is valuable for young dogs. Regular feeding and sleeping inside the crate lets your dog know this is their safe and secure space, especially if you regularly take them out to the toilet in the appropriate place in the yard, grass or synthetic grass trays. If your dog toilets in the crate, the punishment is straightforward and undesirable, and they are likely not to repeat the behaviour.

If crate training is a regular and consistent practice, it serves as a psychologically safe and secure place for your dog, which helps build independence away from you. This is useful in preventing and managing separation-related problems because your dog knows the area and can remain calm and relaxed knowing they will be let out to play, train, walk and relax with you.

When transporting your dog in the car, a crate is a very safe and secure place where your dog won't be jumping up and down, causing distractions for you while driving. It's also better to have your dog contained in one spot in case of an accident.

I keep the crate in the back of the canopy of my Ute (pickup truck), for when I am travelling with multiple dogs. If they are wet and dirty, I like to have them in the crate until I can clean him. If you must transport your dog via aircraft or a pet delivery service, your dog must travel in a transport crate for that duration.

When on holiday and you are in the position to bring your dog with you, the crate can be beneficial as you can contain your dog securely without running the risk of destructive behaviour or escaping from the rental property. The consistency of a crate can also ensure your dog feels safe and secure limiting the likelihood of separation distress.

Crate training is essential if you need to manage anxious, fearful, or aggressive dogs. This allows you to control the situation, improve your training and behaviour modification process, and maintain the safety and security of your visitors from the aggressive behaviour your dog may display.

When you have several visitors over, such as a party occupying both the inside and backyard of your home or if you have tradespeople at your house for a job, putting them in the crate during the duration allows you to maintain control and keep your dog secure. This management is not only for maintaining the safety from aggressive behaviour or giving your dog a safe place away from 'scary' visitors, but also keeping your dog from escaping your property if a visitor may accidentally leave doors or gates open in the busy times of a party or construction-type situations.

Dogs living in apartments should be crate trained, especially when raising a puppy or young dog. This does not mean you need to adhere to crating daily and forever, but at least the first 6-12 months to develop the conditioning and the ability to put your dog in the crate at any time you need to in the years to come.

Usually, dogs spend the nighttime sleeping inside their crate or at random times of the day when you need them to have some downtime away from the busy schedule of family life, etc. There are no set rules for when your dog should be crated as this depends on your requirements and lifestyle. However, we should not leave dogs in crates for periods longer than 8 hours. For example, they shouldn't be crated at night for sleep and again when at work, otherwise your dog lives in a crate for more time than they are out of the crate. This is not an ideal or appropriate way of life. You can have your dog crated at night time and spend time in the yard, courtyard or access to part of the house during the day. Alternatively, your dog can crated during the day while you work and is let out in the yard, courtyard or home for the afternoon and night time for sleeping.

Crate training gets your dog used to confined spaces and is beneficial if your dog needs to stay in a kennel or vet-holding cage. These places can be stressful at the best of times, so teaching your dog to be okay with a crate can set them up for future unforeseen events. When dogs have significant injuries or are recovering from surgery, they may be required to stay inside a crate for prolonged periods for healing. If you have crate trained your dog before this unforeseen event, you are minimising extra stress and anxiety for that time.

General steps to start crate training

All dogs are different, and this is a general guide. Remember, you may find it easier or harder depending on your dog's experiences with a crate and your level of observation, time, and patience. If you need help with the steps below, seeking further help or applying additional techniques may be required.

- Purchase a crate large enough for your dog to stand and turn around a full circle inside the crate, not too large that you could fit two dogs. If your crate is too large for your dog's size, it may be likely that they can poop or pee on one end and sleep on the other end.

- If you know your dog will grow up to fit the larger crate, use a partition (usually included with the crate) to adjust the size your dog has access to until you can allow more space.

- Ensure it is a strong metal crate (not a soft material crate) so that your dog cannot escape.

- Put bedding or a rubber mat on the crate's floor to stop potential slip hazards. If your dog slips the first few times going inside the crate, it may create an aversive event that will likely create a fear response to going inside.

- Keep the door open with a rope and clip to secure it open so it doesn't close on your dog as they enter or exit the crate, which may also create an aversive event for your dog. If the door closes on your dog, and they react negatively, building confidence and trust in the exercise will take longer.

- Place food in a bowl or scattered on the crate floor for the first few days, teaching your dog to go in as they please to be fed their food for the day. Do not physically force your dog to go inside, as this may make them fearful of the whole exercise. Your dog should only gain access to their food by entering the crate on their own accord. Be patient.

- Once your dog is happy and willing to enter and exit the crate on their own accord to eat the food on its floor, you can start to lure them inside the crate. Luring your dog inside the crate is the beginning step to putting a command on going inside the crate.

- MARK + REWARD every effort for going into the crate until you can lure your dog in and reward multiple times for staying inside the crate until releasing ('OK') your dog out of the crate.

- When you have achieved luring your dog in and your dog waiting 30 seconds staying inside the crate for random rewards until being released, you can begin to close the door of the crate. Begin with closing the door (not locking it) and reward multiple times (5 seconds) before opening it and releasing your dog from the crate. Add the verbal command 'CRATE' before luring your dog inside the crate.

- Gradually build the duration the door can be closed by incrementally extending the duration by doubling the time at every 10/10 success rate. For example, when the dog is comfortable with 5 seconds ten times in a row, close the door for 10 seconds, then close the door for 20 seconds, etc.

- While you are building the duration of the door being closed, you can place your dog's meal in the crate and close the door while they eat, and let them out when they finish.

- You mustn't let them out while they are barking or scratching at the door, which may make it challenging to adhere to the time limit mentioned above. Start with less duration and build gradually, and if they don't start to bark and force themselves out, be patient and wait until your dog is calm.

- If you immediately open the door when your dog is pushing, barking, or scratching to get out, you have reinforced the behaviour and may teach your dog that that specific behaviour lets them out of the crate. You want to teach your dog that a calm demeanour is what gives them the freedom to be let out.

- Once you extend your duration to 10 minutes of being inside the crate with the door closed, you can create some distance between yourself and the crate by walking around the room and rewarding intermittently calm and relaxed behaviour. Placing the crate in the living room or a space you are occupying will help with this.

- Stay consistent with this practice until your dog is happy to stay 30-45 minutes inside the crate while you are present before leaving the room entirely. Generally, once you have achieved 1 hour of your dog being calm and relaxed in the crate, you can significantly compound the time inside the crate. However, the first 60 minutes may be the most difficult.

- Some dogs take to being inside a crate much easier than others, especially if breeders conditioned the crate from a young puppy.

- For bedtime rituals, putting the crate next to your bed when it is time to go to sleep will help as your dog knows you are close by, and you may need to regularly (every 3-4 hours) take them out to go toilet and bring them back into the crate to go to sleep. Over a week of this consistent practice, you can extend the duration to 4-5 hours until your dog can sleep the whole evening before being let out to toilet in the appropriate location.

Enrichment

Enrichment is the addition of specific activities within your dog's environment and lifestyle that help fulfil your dog's biological needs. When dogs interact with these activities voluntarily, it will help meet their psychological and physical needs, which allow them to experience less stress and boredom, especially when left alone. Activities usually involve food and destructive behaviour (with items we choose for them to destroy) so that they have things to do when they spend time alone.

If you do not provide items for your dog to interact with in their yard, kennel or space in the house, they will likely destroy and ruin furniture, skirting, boardings, etc. or become anxious and start barking, howling and trying to find a way out to find you.

When utilising the items mentioned below that involve food, it is best to incorporate their daily ration of food to prevent overfeeding and increase your dog's likelihood of interacting with the enrichment item.

Raw food is a big part of my dog's daily ration of food. I typically use kibble or dog roll with obedience training as it is easy to handle and take with me when I am out and about. The raw food portion is simply half defrosted and put inside 2 or 3 KONG™ toys and given to my dogs which takes them four times longer to consume the food, which provides them with something to do and fulfils the instinctive side of their brains.

Naturally, dogs are social predators; they hunt for food in packs. In our domestic environment, dogs do not hunt and kill for their meal, so when you use these types of enrichment strategies, it helps surrogate the natural ways a dog would eat food by squeezing their mouth into the gaps to get to meat/food as their wild counterparts would and still do by dismembering the prey to consume it.

Ensure in multi-dog households that there are enough items for the dogs to share to prevent resource guarding. If your dog does resource guard, maintain dogs in separate yards or areas when providing enrichment. Never leave items you know your dogs will fight over when you are not present to prevent injury and decrease the likelihood of these types of behaviours repeating.

- When leaving your dogs unattended, you should provide games and activities to stimulate your dog's mind.

- Using products such as the KONG™ is a great tool. It's a rubber toy that is hollow on the inside and can be stuffed with their favourite treats or freezing some of your dog's daily ration of food (raw meat, leftovers or soaked kibble) to help with leveraging the value of the game and keep your dog valuing the food they receive throughout the day. Plenty of different shapes, sizes and brands are found in your local pet store.

- Plastic milk/drink bottles (cut holes into them so they can smell the food and give them a chance to get food out). Eventually, they will learn to destroy the bottle to retrieve the food.

- Nylon bones, deer antlers, goat horns, and other longer-lasting enrichment toys can also be given to your dogs.

- You can also use empty cardboard boxes, stuffed

toys, deflated soccer balls, branches, and other safe things your dog can destroy.

- Raw meaty bones 1-2 times per week, depending on your dog's size, temperament around bones (if they try to swallow whole, resource guarding, etc.) and digestive needs (sensitive to certain types of food). I usually give my medium-large breed dogs chicken carcasses, beef brisket or turkey necks. This is their meal for the day as they consume the entire thing. For my small breed dog, I give chicken wings. All bones must be raw and defrosted in the fridge before feeding to prevent food spoilage and the growth of bacteria.

- Items mentioned above must be safe for your dog. Ensure you supervise your dog when first interacting with these enrichment items to ensure they are not swallowing anything besides the food, as it can become a choking hazard or items that can obstruct the digestive system (oesophagus or intestines).

Muzzle conditioning

Muzzles are a crucial and lifesaving piece of equipment. Using a muzzle is essential if you own a dog that displays aggressive behaviour, even if your dog has only bitten on one occasion. It is valuable to muzzle condition your dog purely to teach a new and challenging exercise along with always being able to muzzle for whatever unforeseen event comes up.

Properly conditioning a dog to wear a muzzle is to help

your dog feel completely neutral and comfortable (physically & mentally) when wearing it. At best, it's for your dog to feel better knowing that good things follow when it is on. If forcing your dog to wear it and strapping it on straight away is your plan, it most likely will work against you. Your dog will be incredibly stressed, which can affect his behaviour and the training program.

Keep in mind that this process may take a couple of weeks to get your dog comfortable to go for a walk or participate in a training session. If your dog is stressed by the sight of the muzzle and wearing it, you risk your dog not displaying the behaviours you may be wanting to fix or suppress food drive which also affects the outcomes of training and behaviour modification. More importantly, your dog will be stressed and unhappy.

Other issues like your dog refusing to wear a muzzle by avoiding, hiding or biting you in extreme cases. So, make muzzle conditioning a part of your training before taking your dogs to high-risk environments so that your dog does not bite others or you. Dogs can unintentionally bite owners while faced with certain stimuli—called redirected aggression.

I use basket muzzles or other robust and reliable cage muzzles to allow the dog to breathe, drink and eat treats easily, and ensure they cannot crush the muzzle to bite someone. Make sure you are using a sturdy, strong muzzle and that buckles/clips are in good condition. Make sure it fits correctly and that your dog cannot bite anything. Some muzzles are unreliable as they are weak and soft and still give the ability to bite someone. Ensure you purchase the best muzzle, as this is an essential line of defence preventing potential liability, injury and even death in some instances.

- Start with the desired muzzle you want your dog to wear.

- Place high-value food in the bottom of the muzzle like a cup. While sitting on a chair, present the muzzle upside down to your dog with your palm covering the bottom where the food is. Once your dog automatically fits their snout entirely in the muzzle, start marking and rewarding duration—i.e., rewarding for one entire second of your dog pushing their nose against the inside of the muzzle while continuously feeding from the outside of the muzzle. This shows your dog that the action of the nose in the muzzle makes the food come.

- Once you get a success rate of 10/10 times, move to 2 seconds duration of your dog's nose inside the muzzle.

- If you are struggling to get your dog to keep their nose/mouth in the muzzle, you can cut the top off with scissors to expose the tip of your dog's mouth/nose while practising this step. This means you must purchase another muzzle to continue moving forward and using the muzzle functionally. If you need to continue the steps with the muzzle that has been modified, this is okay, as long as, at some point, you introduce the intact muzzle in later stages.

- With patience and persistence, you can teach your

dog to keep their nose in the muzzle for up to 7-10 seconds before rewarding. This is when you're ready to proceed to the next step, which is getting your dog used to you touching and moving the straps towards the back of your dog's head.

- When conditioning your dog to you holding the straps, it changes how the muzzle sits on their face, as their head tilts up when your hands change position. Take your time with this point in the process, as your dog may find this extremely uncomfortable and may attempt to remove the muzzle with their paws.

- After you have gotten past the point of your dog allowing you to strap the muzzle on and keep it on for more than 3 seconds, it's time to start getting your dog to move around while wearing it. This is best done at first by luring your dog into basic movements and immediately removing the muzzle after 2 or 3 repetitions. Don't push it too far.

- Gradually start doing lots of training sessions while your dog is wearing the muzzle. Go for short walks with the muzzle on, and have fun times around wearing the muzzle. This is a far better way to positively associate with the muzzle than simply putting it on.

Many variables come into play with muzzle conditioning, so this step-by-step guide should be a foundation you start and head towards.

The biggest mistake is when people rush the process and

their dog has a negative experience with the muzzle. If you don't have the muzzle fitted correctly and your dog successfully removes it, your dog will try harder in the future, which can damage your dog's face or dew claws.

Muzzle conditioning- Initial steps

https://me-qr.com/iAwfOrvd

11
Socialisation

A big misconception about socialisation is that it is only about playing and social behaviour when interacting with one or more dogs in a play environment. This is true, but only an element of socialisation. You must develop your dog's ability to be calm and comfortable to work with you in the presence of other dogs, people, and animals. It is also about creating positive and neutral associations with other beings, e.g., to make people and dogs a less threatening stimulus in your dog's perception and more of a positive feeling and association when seeing either people and dogs. It is essential to learn how to teach your dog when it is appropriate to play and how to play, when to focus on you,, and how to ignore what was once the impulse to chase or engage.

The foundations of socialisation began when your dog was a puppy, particularly in the critical period of development (between the ages of 7- 17 weeks old). What occurs, good, bad, or ugly in this time has a lasting effect on the rest of your dog's life. The most important time for puppy owners is in the critical period of making positive and neutral associations with the world and everything in it.

If you have socialisation issues, either reactive/aggressive behaviour or overexcited behaviour, or your dog shuts down and lays down helplessly or tries to run away does not mean it is too late. I have seen firsthand that even when dogs have these types of issues that it's possible to improve their socialisation. By following a good socialisation plan along with structure, management, and appropriate fulfilment, you can see enormous success. Each dog is different, of course, but with baby steps in the right direction, you can properly socialise him.

Beware of dog parks! Even though they are a great idea in theory, from my personal experience and the experience of others, it can also be a dangerous place for your dog. Many of my clients that I have seen with reactive or aggressive dogs share a similar story. Their dog was well socialised until one day at the dog park, another dog attacked them. Since that experience, the dog has been lunging and reactive to other dogs, generally caused by fear. This happened to me and my 6-month-old dog, Spades, in 2011.

I know this doesn't happen to everyone, and some may say that their dog park has been great and their dog has never been involved in any adverse incidents. However, since no one with proper experience and knowledge supervises the dog park, things can get out of hand quickly, or an aggressive dog may enter the park and, with no apparent warning, attack another dog. It could also be that your young dog with limited socialisation with a group of dogs becomes overwhelmed and stressed by an excited, happy-go-lucky larger dog. It does not need to be a vicious attack to be perceived as an aversive event by your dog. If your dog has a bad experience like this, especially when they are young (under six months old), it can have a lasting negative impact.

Effects can range from anxiety, aggression, reactivity, and antisocial behaviour.

If you decide to take the risk and responsibility of going to a dog park, try to go less regularly (once a fortnight), and give your dog free play at the dog park in the middle of your walk (20/20/20 rule). Park your car three blocks away from the off-leash area so that you can walk back and forth from the park. Usually, the larger dog parks (fence-free) compared to the standard smaller fenced areas (mosh pits) are safer. The more space, the better. Keep moving when in the off-leash area; your dog must be following you the whole time while still playing and engaging with other dogs. Standing in one spot usually causes issues with dogs as they all assemble around their owners where fights can usually occur for many reasons, such as resource guarding and fearful behaviour as your dog tries to seek protection and safety of you.

If the other dog continues to pursue and you do not do anything, your dog may lunge and bite in the act of defensive aggression. Playing that goes out of hand without owner intervention can also cause a dog fight. The dynamics are complex, so novice owners should avoid dog parks.

Dog parks can also be a place where your dog will learn to ignore you and find that playing with other dogs is way more exciting than you. Play is an essential time of a dog's life. If you outsource that to other dogs too frequently (daily for some people as the dog park is the only form of exercise for their dog), then that important time does not involve you when out in public and around other dogs. This can result in your dog wanting to run up and play with every dog they see, and even though this seems cute and exciting, it can become an undesirable habit. This habit becomes annoying and potentially dangerous in the future.

You can alternatively use the dog park to help with your training by setting up a training session on the outside of a dog park fence, where your dog takes notice of all the other dogs inside the off-leash area. At the appropriate distance of the fence line, work on obedience/focus/engagement on you. Your dog must remain on a leash and use this as another resource in your training plan.

Teaching the social side of play will not be covered in great detail here as it is complex and best described while watching dog behaviour, and the environment is critical to understanding body language in real-time. Assessing the dogs before playtime is vital to reducing the risk of a dog attack, bite, or bad experience.

If you like to let your friend's dog play with yours at your house, the best thing to do is meet at the front of your home and go for a walk for at least 20 minutes; before going inside, assess how the dogs are acting towards each other, if all is looking good (positive and mutual) then proceed to go to the yard and let them play off the lead. This sequence of events minimises overexcitement, which makes play more likely to be mutual and also gives you an assessment of how the dogs are together in neutral territory. Ensure the yard is free of food, bones, and other high-value items that dogs may try to guard and potentially fight over.

Bringing a dog straight into the yard before letting them meet and establishing a unit or pack can make one dog irritated or fearful when you get the other dog into the yard unannounced. Think about it, bringing the energy of the yard from 0-100 is too much for a smooth interaction (unless the dogs know each other very well and have played previously).

Play time should be a mutual activity for all dogs involved and supervised for the first few times with all new dogs involved. You should be able to establish boundaries for all the dogs to help teach them if they are playing in an undesirable way. Dogs will and should be able to express their boundaries by using body posturing, social corrections, and establishing social skills in these play times.

Dogs are social creatures, and play is an integral part of the dog's life, especially with other pack members. In our domestic terms, a pack means who lives in your family. In wild terms, generally, it's who is in the dog family. Your dog does not need to play with random dogs, your dog needs to play and work with you. As owners and handlers, we provide the most significant amount of play with our dogs.

To play with friends and family dogs is, of course, a great thing if all the dogs are known to be friendly, social, and an appropriate size and age for the group of dogs. Some dogs don't know when it is too much and will miss social cues from the other dogs. Therefore, supervision is essential, especially with higher drive and larger breeds. When you start to see when one has had enough and wants to rest or do something else, but the other dog does not know how to read that body language, you must intervene to teach the dog what that means when the dog displays a particular body language to stop the game at that moment.

When dogs play, their owners are leaders and can control

and direct any dogs when appropriate; if the dog is familiar and comfortable with you, common sense applies. Injury can occur when a dog is not used to playing for long durations, often observed when we used to provide dog minding services for some years. So, if the dogs are tiring, give them time to chill by working on your BED command and separating them into different yards or crates.

While dogs play, practising recall and other obedience training are helpful. This improves impulse control and your commands. You may need leads attached to the dogs and run loose while they're playing. You may also need to use the leash to follow through with commands if your dog ignores you. This is particularly important if your time with friends is a whole day event, and your dog needs to learn how to settle with the group where you can practice time to chill and to be settled when you see it is necessary. After a relaxed time of 30-45 minutes or after they wake up can be an excellent time to let your dog out to be with everyone again.

When on a short lead and a walk, I rarely let my dogs interact with other dogs. I always want to keep the short leads for work and focus, not for playing with other dogs; this is why the 20/20/20 rule works. While my dog is on the long lead or off the lead in the middle of the walk, they have earnt the free time to play and have free time before returning home. The walk-on short lead is a job, not a holiday.

If you're introducing a puppy to your existing pack or your individual dog, remember that you think your puppy is super cute, but your dog or other dogs may not agree. It's common for your older dog to accept a puppy initially only partially, even if the pup is playful. To ensure a safer and more positive interaction, as always, have a good management plan in place. The puppy should always be on the lead, and your older dog should be free to roam if there are no aggression issues in your older dog. Show that you're in control and represent all dogs. The pup should have its their own space (exercise pen and crate) so that after good and positive interactions, you have a place to finish on a successful, positive note and not cause unnecessary stress.

Not all dogs are social, and if your dog gets into the habit of running up to every dog they see, your dog could get bitten! It can affect your training, particularly the recall and general obedience when in the presence of other dogs (going for a walk, enjoying a meal at the coffee shop, etc.). Remember you want your relationship with your dog to be based on fun, trust, respect, and enjoyment. Ensure you're the favourite thing in your dog's life.

When out on a walk remember the following:

- It is unnecessary to say 'hi' to any dog you walk past. Teach your dog to be calm when seeing other dogs.

- Keep them focused on you using treats, the 'LOOK' command, and your basic obedience training.

- Do you speak to and touch every person you pass by when out and about? If not, don't expect it to apply to your dog's interactions with others.

- I generally recommend no on lead greetings with other dog. If you do, keep them from playing. Their leads will get tangled, which is annoying and may result in a negative experience. Remember, we want to encourage calm interactions, not excitement, with every dog you encounter.

- Cross-check the intro to dogs and socialisation as there are repeated themes.

Introducing dogs

When introducing two or more dogs together, it is easy for things to get out of hand very quickly, which may lead to an undesirable outcome, such as a dog fight or creating an adverse situation for one of the dogs. Misreading a dog's behaviour or assuming things will go smoothly is a prevalent mistake. Even though aggressive behaviour wasn't present, a dog may perceive an isolated experience as adverse enough to create fear or insecurity, which can quickly become the beginning of behavioural issues. Over-excitement in dogs can also lead to unfortunate outcomes, so setting your dog up for success is essential when introducing them to other dogs.

Following a few protocols is essential to ensure a safe, friendly, and enjoyable experience for all involved. It isn't always as easy as unleashing a few dogs in the backyard or letting dogs sniff on the lead, and suddenly, they are best friends.

This is not about addressing a dog park or a leash-free park situation, this section is about managing friends' and family's dogs (not random dogs), playing and being around each other on a property, or playing in the park (on or off leash).

Before considering your dog to have off-leash play or to be around other dogs in close proximity, it is helpful to ask yourself a few questions:

- What is the purpose of my dog being free with other dogs?
- Are all the dogs well-mannered and appropriately socialised?
- Is my dog ready or fit to be around dogs in an off-leash situation?
- Will my dog be too overwhelming for the other dog or puppy?
- Has my dog been attacked or had undesirable interactions with dogs?
- Has my dog ever displayed aggressive behaviour towards other dogs?

The best practice is to walk dogs on a loose lead for a 15- to 30-minute period, following their owner, on neutral ground. Ideally, each dog is appropriate on lead, giving full focus to their handler/owner, and begins to ignore the other dog. Walking to a park and attaching dogs on a long lead (keeping the long lead short to start) allows the dogs to sniff and engage with each other. When it comes time for the dogs to have a physical interaction, ensure both handlers of the dogs are on opposite sides to each other and maintain that position in case the dogs need to be separated immediately (12 o'clock and 6 o'clock position—think of a clock drawn on the floor). If all things look mutual and dogs are happy to engage in play or do their own thing and ignore each other, then we know that there is excellent potential for them to accept being around each other.

When letting dogs off the lead in a common area, such as somebody's backyard, ensure there isn't food or other potentially highly valued resources present to minimise any potential for resource guarding. It is also essential to supervise the dogs if it is their first or second time being free to play, to make sure that all dogs are being respectful of each other and that all dogs involved are paying attention to each other's body language. Suppose one of the dogs has had enough, whether tired or overwhelmed, and is displaying this body language to another dog, but the other dog doesn't receive it well or misses the cue. In that case, you must be there to allow all dogs to feel safe and represent all the dogs in that area.

Social corrections (e.g., lip raising, body posturing, and barking) are normal social canine behaviour, a way to communicate that what behaviour is currently being displayed must stop. If one of the dogs does not understand or is ignoring these social cues, we must take responsibility and help communicate this to the dog that is not understanding these cues. We allow dogs to communicate naturally, but we do not want dogs to fight or display unnecessary dominant behaviour. We are the leaders of the pack or group of dogs and set the rules.

If dogs are overtired and play has become annoying or adverse to one of them, we must stop the play and give dogs a break (if they cannot facilitate this on their own). Either separate them on another side of a gate, tether them on another side of the yard, or finish the play session on a positive note by leaving. It's best to ensure the dogs have had an excellent time to allow for a positive experience in future meetings.

Not all dogs want to play or interact with other dogs, this is very important to understand. You and your dog are the pack, and just because you are friends with other dog owners does not mean that your dog will want to play or engage with your friend's dog. This can be for many reasons, such as fear-related issues, un-desexed male dogs tend not to want to share the same space, and previous undesirable experiences with dogs. Respect this and adjust your expectations to the dog you have, not to the dog you used to own or the expectation you set because of how other dogs behave with other dogs.

12

Behaviour Modification

Desensitisation

In psychology, desensitisation is a treatment or process that diminishes emotional responsiveness to a negative, aversive, or positive stimulus after repeated exposure.

You will often hear the word desensitisation throughout your training; it is a big part of behaviour modification, socialisation, and habituation to ensure your dog feels comfortable around certain things, people, animals, or different environmental stimuli. If your dog likes to chase and bite the tyres of a bicycle and we want to stop them from doing this, your goal is to desensitise your dog to bikes zooming past. Changing your dog's perception and thus their behaviour when in the presence of bikes allows the dog to feel calmer and neutral to bikes.

You will be making progress towards desensitisation through specific techniques such as counter conditioning, good management like choosing the correct environment specific to your dog, and effective control by utilising the proper equipment.

To effectively desensitise your dog to specific things, you must control your dog's exposure to the stimulus. If you are trying to desensitise your dog to the presence of other dogs and are working diligently while in sessions on the leash, you may make some progress with your dog's reactivity to other dogs. However, if your leaving your dog in the front yard unattended and he's rehearsing barking at other dogs, you will not be able to truly desensitise your dog to other dogs.

Systematic desensitisation

Systematic desensitisation is a form of desensitisation in which you progressively expose your dog to a particular stimulus and incrementally increase the distance, duration, or intensity of that stimulus over a period of time.

When it comes to systematic desensitisation, knowing and noting the critical distance between your dog and the trigger is essential. This stimulus creates a conditioned response in your dog that you want to change. That critical distance is the maximum distance the stimuli (trigger) can be before a reaction is displayed. Systematic desensitisation aims to incrementally decrease the distance between the dog and stimuli by creating a new conditioned response in the dog that we have expressly set out to teach and train.

Another way desensitisation can occur is when the stimulus randomly occurs in the environment, and over time, naturally, the dog does not take notice of that stimulus. This can be when a dog is re-homed and comes from the country where they did not hear police sirens at all, and in the first week of owning the new dog, you notice the dog goes crazy at the sound of the sirens and starts to bark and howl. A month goes by, and you see the dog ignoring the sirens without any assistance through training.

Usually, the best practice with systematic desensitisation is to create a list. Write the end result at the bottom of the page and list backyards what you need to do. At the top of the list is where you are currently with your dog's behaviour. Writing the goal and progressive steps makes it easier to know how to desensitise your dog to a particular stimulus rather than going into it headfirst with no direction. Suppose you do not know what you're aiming at in a session. In that case, your dog will find it very hard to understand what you're trying to communicate, mainly because you are usually desensitising your dog to something that makes them fearful, stressed or overly excited. It can be hard to maintain a level of focus.

Baby steps to success rather than giant leaps of failure. Incremental and specific steps along a training plan are best. A well-thought-out plan gives your dog good direction in keeping training clear, concise, and enjoyable. Systematic desensitisation is the process in which your dog will substitute the undesirable behaviour for a conditioned response, neutral or good, using counter-conditioning.

Counter conditioning

Counter conditioning is a technique that focuses on changing a conditioned response to a particular stimulus to a new and specific conditioned response when encountering the same stimulus.

This process is integral to behaviour modification and changing your dog's mindset to a more desirable one. You can teach, train and further create a desirable conditioned behaviour to replace an undesirable behaviour in the presence of a trigger. For example, if your dog is looking at you, it is hard to lunge towards a bike zooming by at the same time. Furthermore, if your dog is compelled to look at you as a reflexive response to the stimuli (the bike), this, in turn, changes the undesirable behaviour to a more desirable one by changing the dog's feelings to the stimuli. This is the definition of counter conditioning.

Our goal when counter conditioning is to create a reflexive and emotional feeling in the dog to achieve desensitisation. This is important to know when fixing the lunging toward a bike. At first, we teach the dog to look at us when we give the command until at a safe enough distance (just outside the critical distance), your dog can perform the behaviour when told.

With good timing and consistency, the dog will look at you at you for food when they see a bike, even without being told the command. This is what it means to counter condition. Your dog didn't think about looking at you; they had the feeling to do so reflexively.

This is the beginning step of counter-conditioning, and the rabbit hole can go quite deep. The thing to take away is that we are trying to change how our dogs feel about the 'trigger' not only to have a sense of physical control. This process can take some time, but if done with practice, patience and persistence, you will have a longer-lasting behaviour.

Using counter conditioning with your behaviour modification process can make this process more pragmatic. It is a reliable and effective option to change behaviour and ultimately desensitise your dog to the stimuli that initially provoked an undesirable response. It should help the dog become more neutral around the particular stimulus so that you can layer in obedience and create rules of engagement in specific situations.

Counter-conditioning techniques teaches your dog to focus on you voluntarily in the presence of the trigger. You want your dogs to focus on you without having to give the 'LOOK' command, but instead to focus on us when things trouble them so we can guide them in the presence of any trigger or undesirable situation.

Example: My dog Chilli's fear of people holding fishing rods and only using counter conditioning:

When I first acquired my dog Chilli, I noticed in the first week that he found anyone holding a fishing rod a threat. From 20 meters away his hackles, tail and ears would stand tall, deep growl and hard stare. I was feeding entirely from my pouch at this stage.

The moment I noticed Chilli's behaviour I did the name game, tapped his leash and said 'Chilli', as soon as he looked me I rewarded handsomely. I repeated this 3 times and left the area.

I ensured I visited the same spot daily and repeated this process. On day three, Chilli noticed a fisherman and he snapped his head to me (without me giving any leash pressure, verbal cue or body language), he associated the fishing rod with food from me. I gave a 'YES' + REWARD as soon as he looked at me—incrementally decreasing the distance between Chilli and the fisherman by 5 meters every

10 repetitions, which took about a week and a half.

The end result was me being able to sit on the bench with Chilli by my side. When a fisherman holding a bucket and rod walked by and Chilli kept looking at him and looking at me rapidly, anticipating a reward, I stopped rewarding soon after.

Now we walk past fishermen at close distance and Chilli shows no acknowledgement of them. This neutral feeling he has achieved is desensitisation through counter conditioning.

Flooding

Flooding is a technique aimed at exposing a stimulus to an individual that triggers a conditioned response (usually used to treat fear/anxiety). The stimulus is presented at a high intensity with no ability to escape until a desired behaviour is displayed. In the hope to desensitise a dog to the fear-inducing stimuli/situation, learning that nothing 'bad' occurred and that stimuli can stop/go away by performing a behaviour we see as desirable.

Sometimes flooding works on its own, for example, a new dog from a country town now lives in a busy suburban area. At first the sounds of nearby cars, construction sites, and neighbours are fear-inducing. But, because these things don't go away and the dog is being fully immersed in them with a high amount of exposure, their negative response goes away. Being flooded initially brings high stress levels, however, if done correctly the dog settles quicker with each exposure. The one trigger starts to be a thing in the background; thus, the dog becomes desensitised.

Flooding used on its own is usually not a go-to technique prescribed, as it has a high failure rate which can often lead to increasing fear/anxiety when faced with a stimulus the next time. This is especially true if you are not aware of the individual dog, their temperament and if you lack experience and have incorrect timing.

For example, if your dog fears people and you force your dog to walk through a busy mall/public walkway, you may achieve success over a few repetitions, or you may make things worse, creating more behavioural issues. This can lead to your dog shutting down (learned helplessness) or reactive and aggressive behaviour.

Real world applications

As much as all this theory is 100% correct, systematic desensitisation and counter-conditioning can be complex when applying the early stages in public spaces. You can't guarantee the other dog will stay at the perfect 6.5 metres away to fit within your dog's critical distance and the training plan.

With this in mind, we still use and plan according to a counter-conditioning process but have the other variables and techniques at play for the safety and management of your dog. Things like leash handling, obedience, the right tools, punishment (if/when necessary,) and confidence building to handle a difficult situation. Also, be clear-minded so you can plan and make space appropriately when navigating any environment.

This is why explaining these concepts is essential and can be helpful for mild to medium behaviour issues, but for more extreme and potentially dangerous behaviour (aggression and anxiety), best to consult with a professional one-on-one.

Mindset and behaviour

A dog's behaviour is a manifestation of their mindset. To change your dog's behaviour, it is usually best to address and alter their mindset, and the only way to do that is by consistently manipulating behaviour in the current moment. How paradoxical!

As a human example goes, if a friend of yours has a panic attack, is hyperventilating, and acting very erratic and unsettled, it is not helpful to yell at them to, 'CALM DOWN'! If anything, this will make matters worse for your friend as the anxiety intensifies. It is much more beneficial to approach your friend calmly, make eye contact and get them to breathe calmly through the nose out the mouth, and count back from 10. You may find the anxiety settles after a minute or so, and your friend is happier for it. This is an example of controlling and manipulating behaviour (what someone is currently doing) to influence mindset. The hard part is you can't tell your dog to yoga breathe, but we can train and condition behaviour via specific training methods.

When a dog is overexcited on a walk, jumping at birds, barking at people, and trying to play with everything around him, the best approach is to adhere to your training plan. Once you have the training collar on in the correct position, walking rules should be kept up, which start inside the house. Training should be practised regularly. This begins with changing your dog's way of thinking from over-aroused to focused and calm. The leash should represent work, focus, and a certain mindset.

By setting up the training session, the environment you choose to walk in and a way of physically controlling your dog via the leash, you are changing your dog's behaviour. Over time, within each session, walk, and situation, you'll begin to change your dog's life and how they see the world. You will see a change in your dog's attitude, which we achieved via conditioning by developing new habits.

You can change your dog's mindset/belief/emotion by changing your dog's behaviour and vice versa. This is key to long-term success in behaviour modification.

Confidence and manners—both sides of the same coin

To have a complete and balanced dog, we ideally like to have a dog with solid confidence and good manners. Experiences of puppyhood, environment, and your dog's genetics determine how confidence and temperament are established as your dog matures.

To have manners, some confidence may be sacrificed; building confidence, some manners may go astray. Better to have reasonable confidence in a young dog than to expect too much manners in the first 8 to 12 months. This certainly does not mean ignoring boundaries or rules for a young dog. It means not expecting too much too soon as you may take away some excellent and necessary confidence/drive that is a part of your dog's character.

Be mindful of how to find this balance, especially for dogs suffering from fear issues. For example, if a dog shows fear and aggression toward me in the first session by barking or avoidance, in the second session, if the dog is more comfortable with me, I will allow him to jump up to say hey to build confidence. We will eventually layer in more rules as time goes by, but if I can praise the confidence peeping through the dog's psyche, I want to celebrate it. Any effort of play is rewarded, which is a precursor to trust and building a relationship.

It can also go the other way. Too much confidence with no manners is what a dog trainer usually gets hired for. Allowing your young dog to live without rules or boundaries, can develop confidence beyond your control which manifests into problem behaviours like barking, destructive behaviour, anti-social/unruly behaviour, and even aggression. We may temporarily take some freedoms away, limit the behaviours through management, offer correction, and develop impulse control, making room for structure, training, and clarity.

This is not about taking away confidence, but somewhat limiting behaviour associated with being overly confident. In the short term, it will restrict the dog's drive and show them where and when it is appropriate to express that state of mind. Confidence and manners are opposites, but both are essential for a dog to function well in our world.

Displacement signals

Displacement signals are normal behaviours displayed out

of fear, stress, conflict, and anxiety in the presence of a stimulus:

- Lip licking
- Yawning
- Paw up
- Whale eye
- Self-grooming
- Sniffing the ground

These behaviours are typically seen when the dog wants to change the outcome of a situation or wants to do something in relation to a stimulus but is suppressing the impulse to do it. Displacement signals (calming signals) are associated with the body language of stressed, anxious or fearful dogs, i.e., ears/tail tucked, raised hackles, panting, laying on back, etc. As dogs are social mammals, body language is a crucial part of communication. These displacement signals are helpful when submitting or appeasement in a social situation that is observable to the other dog.

For humans, stroking hair, biting nails, looking at your phone, and playing with your thumb or ring are all different types of displacement signals that you may perform in stressful or anxious situations. It is a way to stop or avoid a stressful stimulus/ situation through distraction and avoidance.

All are important in context to your dog's standard patterns of behaviour, the situation/environment you are in, and being aware of how your dog responds when stressed. Be in tune and develop the art of observation.

Leash reactivity

Leash reactivity is a commonly used term with a loose definition of behaviour and may mean many different things. When people use the term leash reactivity, it generally means your dog reacts to a particular stimulus or triggers that lead your dog to lunge, bark, jump, and act in a typically undesirable way. Causes for leash reactivity can be a range of reasons, from fear that creates a defensive response which may lead to aggressive behaviour or excitement that leads to your dog being frustrated, aroused, and overstimulated trying to get closer to a desirable thing (e.g., another dog or person). Similar to the excitement, your dog may see prey from a distance and display reactive behaviour due to prey drive, where your dog may want to chase the prey; however, the leash is blocking their access, thus the frustration your dog experiences creates 'leash reactivity'. Either way, it is usually a behaviour that we would like to eliminate. To acquire the desired behaviour in our dog, we first need to identify why we see the 'reactivity'.

A lot of the time, this behaviour has become reinforced by allowing your dog to achieve the response they were seeking. If your dog is overly excited and learns over time to make a big fuss which leads to you allowing them to approach and interact with a dog or person, then your dog learns to do that behaviour for the next time. This is training, just not achieving your desired goals. Remember your dog is always learning, and you are always 'training' when engaging in activities with your dog. If, on some occasions, you allow your dog to greet another dog, especially in an over-excited way, yet on other times you do not allow the interaction, the frustration your dog experiences increases to the point where they will persist with the behaviour and blow up reactively. Intermittent reinforcement is powerful.

Usually, when dogs are fearful of other dogs/people, their reactivity is a way to push the dog away. In the dog's mind, the 'reactivity' is a way to make dogs go away or to stop them from approaching. When your dog's barking causes the other person or dog to go away, your dog's behaviour is reinforced. In other circumstances, the 'reactivity' displays the dog's true intent and they may bite when they get close enough to the stimulus.

Many dogs I see in private training seem very aggressive when on the lead around other dogs or people but do not show the same behaviour when they are off the lead around the same dog or person. This is because when we attach a lead to our dog, we inhibit its natural ability to engage and operate in the environment. **Fight, Flight, and Freeze** response is a normal instinctive reaction when in the presence of an aversive stimulus. Once we remove the dog's ability to do what is natural (display/read appropriate body language, make the desired space to assess the situation, and 'flight' if they feel threatened), we may see the dog choose a different response (fight- lunge, bark) if they are being 'forced' to walk by a dog or any other stimulus for that matter.

The most unnatural thing we do to our dogs is put them on a lead. With this being said, it is most appropriate to teach our dogs how to operate on a lead, and condition them to behave appropriately by offering them a sense of control that we find suitable and desirable. This is for safety, sociability, and relationship building.

We want our dogs to learn to be social in all aspects. This includes being calm and comfortable around dogs, people, and other stimuli by focusing on their handler and being able to acknowledge another dog without being reactive. It is also appropriate for them to learn how to play with dogs that are part of their 'pack' or social structure, but being able to play with all dogs isn't reasonable. This is a great misconception that's important for all dog owners to understand.

We need to be able to read our dog's body language, have situational awareness, and be able to represent our dog. If your dog is feeling threatened or stressed as an off-lead dog is running straight up to you and your dog, you must try and succeed in showing your dog that you will handle it, one way or another. Trust is essential, and our dogs need to know that we understand them (by knowing their behaviour patterns) and will protect them from people, dogs, and things around them. If we are unsuccessful with this, your dog will attempt to defend themselves (and maybe you), which is another reason behind leash reactivity.

Here are some steps to take when your dog is reactive to other dogs. This reaction is expressed by barking and lunging toward other dogs:

- Always keep your dog on the lead when off your property, using the appropriate collar and lead for safety and effective leash handling.

- Practice your engagement and obedience training on the footpath out the front of your house. Ensure your dog knows how to follow commands outside their comfortable environment (inside your home or backyard). If your dog cannot follow commands in public when there isn't a dog around, there is very little chance they will follow when fearful, stressed, and over aroused.

- You must know the critical distance (the comfortable distance between your dog and another dog) without seeing reactive behaviour. While at a comfortable distance from another dog, practice the counter-conditioning technique. Also, practising the Name Game, by lighty applying pressure on leash while saying your dog's name and the LOOK command will help bring focus to you. Then you can give your dog extra commands such as Down-Stay or Come. Obedience training should be practised continuously for behavioural modification success.

- If your dog is too stressed to eat food during training, start making your dog eat all their meals via a treat pouch outside of the house before continuing. Teach them to work for their food rather than refusing training food to eat for free in the bowl at home.

- Along with practising these techniques, what is most important is that you maintain the rules of the walk. Keeping up with the rules of the walk is a structured way to teach your dog to follow you and to be less engaged with all the activities in the environment around them. Best that your consequences, good or bad, come via the structured walk so that if your dog were to react to a specific stimulus, you are correcting your dog for breaking the rules of the walk, not because they are reacting to the stimulus depending on the situation. Best to have a professional to show you how to do this if you are feeling overwhelmed, stressed, and confused.

Fearful dogs and confidence building

Fear can cause many problem behaviours in our dogs and can be caused by:

- Lack of early socialisation and habituation
- Single event learning
- Genetic influence

Your dog's fear of certain things, whether of other dogs, people, or environmental stimuli, can cause behavioural issues such as aggression, avoidance, anxiety, and health issues. Only treating the visible behaviour may suppress the undesirable response but not correct what's at the heart of the problem. For example, if your dog is lunging at people coming to your house, you can change the behaviour through training, but a deeper problem may need to be addressed.

The saying 'knowledge is power' is such a relevant concept for dogs that lack confidence and are fearful. Most species fear what they do not know as part of natural survival and creates self-preservation behaviours to feel safe when faced with a particular threat. A lot of behaviours that a dog displays when scared are self-reinforcing, which means the behaviour itself creates the desired outcome for the dog. For example, when your dog barks at someone walking past the front gate of your property, most dogs believe it was their barking and overt behaviour which kept the person from engaging them and keeping them off their property. Or when a dog hides under the bed when somebody comes to your house, it keeps them feeling safe. If your dog finds this successful, the behaviour will repeat.

Better to systematically desensitise your dog (gradual positive baby steps) to make your dog feel good in the presence of the stimulus rather than tell them off because their behaviour is frustrating to you or to overcompensate and nurture your dog every time things get tough without dealing with the cause of the fear directly. Showing your dog how to perceive threats differently or change their behaviour for better outcomes is a good thing. This is when we give our dogs the power to make their own decisions that suit our agenda and allow our dog to experience less unnecessary stress, and as a result, a better life.

Engagement training is a great way to build your dog's confidence by teaching them that safety and positive experiences come through you as the handler. Developing focus on you and your activities is a way in which your dog learns to look at you for direction rather than being burnt out and focusing on everything else in the environment. Training the 'Name Game', 'LOOK', 'RECALL', and Durational commands will alter your dog's mindset to better their situation by making desirable space from the threat without the undesired behaviour. Throughout the training process, the once-perceived threat will become less threatening and more neutral; this takes practice, patience, and persistence.

Teaching your dog what to do when feeling scared allows your dog to control the outcome without extra conflict by displaying dangerous or anti-social behaviour. Making sure you plan what you want your dog to do and not focus so much on what you don't like allows you to be proactive and further increases your dog's trust towards you and the situations you allow to happen. Stress affects learning in ways that make it extremely difficult for your dog to progress significantly. Therefore, having a good management plan and a great set of obedience, leash handling, and, of course, a strong marker in place is critical. It's best to set your dog up for success by not overexposing your dog to the stimuli that elicit the undesired response. Instead, take the time to carefully set up training sessions or scenarios that allow your dog to feel a sense of confidence.

By having a great management plan, you have already started the process on the right foot if you have been working on clear communication via training and leash handling. This makes it easier for you to tell your dog what to do and extend their initial engagement and focus. With a controlled and measured approach and with the above concepts put into practice, you can make small successful sessions to show your dog that the perceived threat is not what was initially perceived. Always finish sessions on a positive note and move away from the environment in which the fear eliciting stimulus is or make the person/dog/thing move away on a high note of the experience.

Knowing when to put your dog in a secured area of the house, whether that is the backyard, a crate, or other designated areas, minimises and eliminates any potential issues accidentally occurring. This is to be used when the training session is over, when you are not in a position to control the situation, or if you are not present when a certain stimulus is present. This is a big game changer, regardless of how good you have been progressing with building confidence in your dog when you are around. If you don't set up your dog for success, you will risk the undesired outcomes to repeat. Keeping your dog in a secure area is not cheating if they fear guests in the house and you are busy cooking or entertaining. Best to bring your dog around the triggers when you are prepared to continue your training. People have made big mistakes by adopting the attitude 'She'll be right' or 'Let the dog figure it out'. If you know your dog doesn't cope well, allow them to trust you and your space to build confidence in the future.

If your dog is fearful of people, clearly express to them not to touch, look, or speak to your dog and not feel embarrassed or ashamed that you need to take control of the situation. If you have your dog's back and show them you are in control, you will more likely maintain a good relationship with your dog when in uncomfortable situations. If your dog fears other dogs, make sure you are in a controlled environment with your dog on the lead so that you can prevent anything from happening.

It is crucial to get to know your dog by studying their body language and behaviour patterns in certain situations and having a relationship based on exercise, play, training, and affection. The more activities, training, and boundary setting you have in your dog's life, the more you are working together, which means you learn communication skills, habits, and attitudes, which is priceless in trust building. Also, don't forget to hang out and have fun with your dog. Everything doesn't have to be a structured activity.

Play is a great way to build confidence in many ways by developing a straightforward and fun game. Fetch and tug are the obvious ones. However, not all dogs are into those types of games; other forms of play are personal play (roughhouse play between you and your dog) and food games (which look like an enjoyable luring activity). Play strengthens your bond, encourages moments of challenge and a way to overcome the challenge, and offers an opportunity to focus on your training and not all the things around him.

Danger is very real, but fear is a choice. This saying gives us leaders some perspective. Your dog may think the person coming through the front door is a danger, and maybe through past experiences, something similar has resulted in a bad experience that triggered trauma. However, our dogs must learn the difference between what is truly dangerous and what is not. Making your dog feel good around certain things takes more than just a good experience. The best way to combat fear in dogs is early socialisation, habituation, and setting your young pup for success in all environments. Understandably, this is not the best remedy if you currently own an adult dog with fear issues.

Genetics play a big part in this, and usually, it is the experiences that turn on certain genetic expressions. We cannot control the dog's DNA (unless we are personally breeding), so we can only lead our dogs appropriately through life, so they adapt to the environment in which we live.

If your dog is genetically nervous and fearful, you may notice similar behaviours in your dog's parents or litter mates. This does not change your training dramatically, but it should change your expectations and approach. Fear is complex and takes time and commitment to build a solid behaviour modification plan. Our fundamental goal in resolving fear-based behaviour is to build confidence, develop good management plans, and train consistently. Relationship building and establishing boundaries are essential for this process. Knowing that you may never eliminate fear and anxiety is helpful, but we can teach our dog coping mechanisms to deal with the world.

How quickly did they recover?

When dealing with behavioural issues, remember that you aim to make small, successful steps toward your desired goal, which would be a calm, well-mannered, and social animal. You need to see these steps as broken-down pieces of a puzzle and be mindful to reinforce even the most minor amounts of effort to what you are trying to teach and train your dog how to do or respond.

If your dog is fearful and you are on the journey to improving her life, to experience the world without stress and anxiety, we must be able to assess progress. You won't be training and seeing immediate results in one day or week. If your dog initially took one minute to recover mentally from a loud sound of a nearby construction site while on a walk, and now three weeks later, your dog takes 10 seconds to recover with your help and guidance, this is a massive success in your training. Do not see failure by thinking, 'After three weeks, they are still scared of the loud sounds.' Think more along the lines of, 'After three weeks, I'm able to help my dog focus on me after scary things, rather than her spending that time trying to run away from everything!'

Once you see your dog's recovery time decrease around specific triggers, you will notice in time to come that the recovery time between encountering the trigger and coming back to baseline becomes so small that you will observe that the reaction to stimuli becomes intermittent. We tend only to notice the undesirable behaviour and forget to focus on how our dog is trying to manage their emotions under challenging scenarios. Be mindful of recovery times, as this is the gateway to achieving success in building confidence for your dog.

Aggression issues

Living with an aggressive dog in any capacity can be incredibly stressful, challenging, and dangerous. Aggression comes in different forms and can be an overly complex issue for most dog owners to identify, manage, treat, and resolve independently. I will cover limited aspects of aggression in dogs. Still, it is highly recommended that you seek professional help from a reputable balanced dog trainer to undergo one-on-one, in-person behaviour modification for your dog with aggression-based behaviours.

Aggression can be displayed by your dog to other dogs but entirely social with humans, and visa-versa, aggressive to people but social with other dogs. You may also see that your dog is happy to hang around people and dogs but will chase and kill the neighbour's cat, or your dog is 100% social with all beings in any capacity, but if you try and take the bone off the dog, they can display aggressive behaviour and bite you. These examples show just how complex aggression is. We will NOT go through a step-by-step process, nor will we cover any specific technique or program to undergo as each case varies. It is far too deep for the scope of this book and best to have a trained professional to guide you based on your and your dog's specific needs. Safety for all involved is at risk when you address these complex, dangerous behaviour problems without clear professional guidance.

Aggression is an instinctive behaviour in dogs that either keeps them safe if they are feeling fearful of a specific threat (defensive); if they are to establish social order (dominance;) or to maintain a resource for themselves such as food, toy, person, etc. (resource guarding). In most pet dogs, dominant aggression can and does exist. However, it is less common to encounter in my experience. Most aggression I have dealt with is more often fear-based aggression and resource guarding but can still have hazardous outcomes.

There is a clear distinction between your dog biting your neighbour for coming through the back gate and your dog chasing the neighbour's cat and killing it (Aggression vs Predation). Predation is a normal canine instinct (aka, prey drive) and is described as the motivation a dog demonstrates to seek, chase, catch, and consume prey. Aggression is an aversive/defensive behaviour, and predation is an appetitive behaviour. All dogs possess predatory instinct and, on their own, does not make a dog 'aggressive'.

Making this clear distinction is merely for your education, and just as the drive/motivation differs between aggression and predation, the stimulus that triggers the behaviour can vary. Managing a dog with aggression or predation issues still requires a similar management model (but not the same) before behaviour modification, and rehabilitation can take place.

Help your dog meet their behavioural goals by managing your dog in all circumstances when in the presence of the stimulus that elicits the aggressive behaviour so that you don't create a situation or make the behaviour stronger (self-reinforced).

For example, if you know your dog fears people and has bitten somebody in the past, your primary call to action is to make sure your dog does not practice biting again. Keep your dog on a lead when out in public; crate your dog when people come over and muzzle your dog when near people and dogs or in populated areas (if you are at that point in your training program). Also, use appropriate equipment for handling and safety—the list goes on. Some call this common sense, but making management part of your primary requirement for living with your dog needs to become a habit without question.

Most dogs that attack someone or get into a fight with other dogs are usually matters of inadequate management and bad timing. Owners typically follow some form of management protocol. Still, it is the one time you let the dog pee out in the front yard unleashed when the situation unfolded, or the dog slipped out of their loose flat buckle collar. I hear stories like this weekly, and these situations can be avoided!

When I am called out to help owners with an aggressive dog in any capacity, I always start all training programs by:

- Charging a food reward marker ('YES').

- Teaching basic commands (SIT, DOWN, COME, BED, LOOK).

- Loose lead walking.

- Establishing rules in the house.

- Understanding dog body language.

- Having appropriate, solid, and fitted equipment.

- Addressing all areas of a dog's life, like their health, lifestyle, owner relationship, what the leash represents, and understand specific triggers the dog may have.

When you don't teach the solid foundation of following basic obedience commands and understanding leash etiquette, it will be exceedingly difficult to be the effective leader your dog needs you to be. Give your dog a job, provide appropriate biological fulfilment, and teach them that when the leash is on, it is work time, not holiday time. Teach them that there are consequences (desirable & undesirable) for their behaviour, especially while on a leash, and be consistent with all your routines in and out of the house. Be diligent with your structure and follow your training plans and activities daily. We want to ensure that you and your dog clearly understand what is expected in each interaction. This saves confusion and the likelihood of a reoccurring incident. Over time you will see changes, and naturally, some of the tight boundaries can ease incrementally, only determined by your dog's behaviour and general performance.

Discipline equals freedom

Once owners start their training journey to address aggression problems in their dogs, many are surprised with how much they enjoy their time with their dogs because their communication skills improve. Therefore, their dogs understand how to avoid the threats they see around them. When aggression is fear-based, you must focus more on building confidence in the dog, not punishing every lunge, bark, and growl. We want to teach the dog how to avoid the stimulus and eventually become desensitised to the presence of that stimulus. Depending on the dog, over time, they will be able to experience more freedom and experience less stress when in public or around people and dogs, so aggression is no longer a necessary behaviour your dog needs to rely on.

For example, what if you have a dog that fears people touching them but is comfortable when they are 2-3 meters away? Next time your friend comes over, tell them to meet in front of your house and send a text message, 'NO TOUCH, NO TALK, NO EYE CONTACT TO MY DOG'. Meet out front with your dog on a leash and walk around the block with your friend together, at a safe distance. Enter the house at a reasonable distance and sit comfortably from each other. Your dog may be staring at your friend; make some space, and give the command 'LOOK', 'YES' + REWARD if your dog does so. Finish the interaction positively within five minutes, and put your dog away into a crate or yard. Small and successful training sessions, appropriate management, having a plan, and not letting your ego run the show are great places to start. This is only a general example. It's important to have professional eyes to show you where to start.

If you leave your dog to do whatever they like with little impulse control—no 'job', no regular training/exercise, off lead to do as they please— getting mad at them for poor behaviour and then over-correcting will only lead to increased stress, a break down in your relationship and create more conflict on top of the already bad experience.

Ensure you appropriately use +P (positive punishment, i.e., leash correction). You must respect the technique and use it to truly help the dog make a better decision and not as a way to vent your frustration or exercise your ignorance.

The problem with applying punishment to correct a dog is that it can work well, but an inexperienced person may rely on it too much, which can cause issues like frustration, fear, stress, and conflict in their dog or desensitise the dog to the leash correction which means it loses its value and no longer can be used correctly. This is particularly important when stopping a dog from lunging, barking, and growling because you may stop early warning signs of aggression. Your dog may be harder to read, and most importantly, punishment in the wrong application may add more stress to your dog and make the behaviour worse. This is another reason why hiring someone experienced and reputable is recommended for treating aggression, and just reading about it will never be adequate for addressing behavioural issues like aggression.

You cannot punish fear, it is technically impossible to punish or reinforce an emotion or state of mind; you can only punish or reinforce behaviour.

If a dog bites someone when being touched or 'cornered', you may punish the dog for that behaviour; however, if the behaviour was a reflexive response due to fear, they could not control that behaviour. If, however, the dog made a calculated decision while walking away and, when unprovoked, ran up to the person to bite them, it is appropriate to +P as it was an instrumental decision to display aggression when the dog had the option to continue to make space. These are examples, not a guide. To the inexperienced eye, it may be challenging to determine small yet significant changes in body language and behaviour.

Building a solid and clear relationship with your dog is essential to success with any behaviour modification program. Your leash should not be the only way of communication between you and your dog. This means there are many ways of communicating, whether with a verbal command or body language, to tell your dog to focus on you, that a reward is available, or to communicate a warning for punishment.

Using your leash only to anchor your dog or to stop them from lunging is not enough to fix any behavioural issue. Be the captain of the ship, not just the anchor. Use all your training techniques and things you have learnt throughout training and in this content to be the language you and your dog share. Learn to read your dog's behaviour and body language, be in tune with their behaviour patterns, and be aware of the subtle changes and how they are being affected by what is in the environment. Respect goes both ways, so be mindful of how your dog thinks and feels in any situation.

A big part of dealing with the intensity of dog aggression is that it takes owners off guard, crushes their belief of who their dogs are or what their dog is capable of, and diminishes relationships in many circumstances. It can be quite confronting and triggers deep emotions in many owners. It is essential to accept that you are faced with a dog that displays aggressive behaviour and can cause injury or death to another person, dog, or other animals. The attitude of, 'Oh, it only happened once and hasn't happened since', or 'I take my dog off the lead when no one is around' is unacceptable. If you genuinely want to change your dog's behaviour, you must be diligent in having complete control of your dog before moving forward with 'fixing' the problem.

Another part of accepting your dog for who they are is not expecting them to fit a perfect mould of our expectations. The hard truth is that environment and training is not the only motivating force that gives dogs their drive. It is also their genetics that determines the potential of the dog. This does not mean you dismiss that your dog is aggressive because of their DNA; it just means they lean more towards fight than flight when things get challenging. Yes, this can be a learned behaviour, and many times it is, but every dog is different. Compare your dog to how they were yesterday, do not compare your dog to how another dog is today, 'My friend's German Shepherd never attacks anyone; why is my German Shepherd trying to kill all my visitors'?! Accept your dog's unique traits, and make the appropriate changes to mitigate all risks. More importantly, reassure your dog and teach them what you really want them to do, not just punish unwanted behaviour. Show your dog you control the environment (access to the world). Trusting in you to maintain control is a big thing for your dog!

I highly recommend muzzle conditioning for any dog with aggression issues. Doing this correctly is so important. If you shove a muzzle on your dog's face and strap it on, you will likely cause a negative association with the muzzle, and the second attempt of muzzling your dog will be a challenge! It may take a week or two to properly show your dog that wearing a muzzle is not bad. Follow the steps under the topic' Muzzle Conditioning' so that your dog is comfortable and conditioned to wear the muzzle easily' otherwise, you'll have to prepare for the big wrestle match and the crocodile rolling that follows, which can be stressful for everyone. Once your dog knows how to wear a muzzle, your behaviour modification process will be much safer and gives you a confidence boost knowing your dog cannot hurt anyone.

Aggression can be a learned behaviour and can develop over time as your dog learns that their pushy, dominant, possessive, and over-aroused behaviour successfully achieves what they want. Setting firm boundaries and a way of life is fundamental to minimising potential aggression issues.

Suppose you allow your dog to persist in early negative

behaviours without correcting consistently and strategically. In that case, you risk desensitising your attempt to control and punish the behaviour as the dog matures. I see this often as new owners expecting that the young puppy may 'grow out' of undesirable behaviours, they don't respond with the best possible outcome in mind. While it may be true that the puppy may outgrow the behaviour, it can be a breeding ground for instinctive and dangerous behaviour. For example, if you never set boundaries and allow your young dog, especially a big powerful breed, to jump on you, and bite your limbs/clothes, etc., by 10 to 12 months, it will likely be harder to correct the behaviour. This could cause you significant frustration, especially if your dog tries to bite you and correct *your* behaviour.

This is a breakdown in the relationship and not a very good thing. If being bitten frightens, hurts, and injures you, and you retreat, your dog learns that biting you is compelling; your dog may use the same behaviour in the future (increasing frequency and intensity) to achieve the same result. This breakdown of your relationship needs to be addressed, and I hope the contents of this book give you insight and remedies to better understand some of your dog's behavioural issues.

The most uncomfortable topic to discuss with dog owners is assessing your dog and how their behaviour impacts your life. Doing this sooner rather than later makes it easier for everyone. If your new 8-month-old Bullmastiff shows early signs of aggression towards your 6-year-old Labrador, you have choices but be clear from the beginning about what you're willing to do. One of the options is to manage the dogs and constant supervision when they are together until the issue has been worked on and resolved appropriately by a professional. If you are unwilling or unable to put in the work, it may be best to re-home the young dog to a home suited to their temperament and requirements.

If it is worse than that, and your dog is severely aggressive to people, and your young toddler is at risk, you have an important decision to make. If you have exhausted all other options (seeing numerous experienced trainers/behaviourists, if necessary, medication-assisted behaviour modification plans, etc.) and still have not made much success, and re-homing the dog is not possible due to the severe aggression. If you have exhausted all options of rescue organisations, then euthanasia is the last option. This seldom happens with my clients, but there have been cases where it was the only responsible action to take, always with a heavy heart, done to ensure the safety of other people, especially children.

Living with a dog that has aggression issues can vary from being relatively easy to live with to as bad as ruining people's lives. It should always be taken with the utmost sincerity and seriousness how you choose to manage and rehabilitate the problem behaviour. Make sure you are taking care of yourself while being the best leader and dog owner you can be. Do the best you can and stay persistent. Be strong mentally and physically, and always remember to honour the dog in front of you. Do not project yourself onto your dog.

Final Words

As we come to the end of this book, I hope you feel equipped with the knowledge and tools to build a stronger, more fulfilling relationship with your dog.

If you want to successfully train and create a happy life with your dog, patience, consistency, and clear communication are key. Training is a lifelong journey, not just a destination. Embrace each step, celebrate every success, and enjoy the process of growing together.

To continue learning about dog behaviour and training, tune in to my podcast 'Life With Your Dog', where we break down dog training concepts and guest interviews with other dog trainers around the world.

If you have enjoyed reading this book and have found it valuable to your dog training journey, please take the time to leave a review on Amazon to help others find this book and help change the world, one dog at a time.

Thank you for allowing me to be part of your dog's life. If you get only one thing from this book, let it be this: the best training tool is the love and connection you share with your dog. As you move forward, remember that every interaction with your dog is an opportunity to learn, teach, and connect. Celebrate the small wins, remain patient through challenges, and never forget why you started this journey—to create a life of joy, trust, and mutual understanding.

Wishing you and your dog a lifetime of happiness together.

—Panos Anagnostou

Made in United States
North Haven, CT
11 July 2025